From Paragraph to Essay

Developing Composition Writing

MAURICE IMHOOF

and

HERMAN HUDSON

LONGMAN

LONGMAN GROUP UK LIMITED
Longman House, Burnt Mill, Harlow,
Essex CM20 2JE, England
Associated Companies throughout the world.

First published 1975
Twelfth impression 1988

Produced by Longman Group (FE) Ltd
Printed in Hong Kong

ISBN 0-582-55232-X

Contents

Contents

Acknowledgements

We are grateful to the following for permission to reproduce copyright material:
Thames & Hudson Ltd for an extract from 'The Pre-Columbian Civilizations' from *The First Americans* by G.H.S. Bushnell. We regret we have been unable to trace the copyright holder of the extract from *Basic Principles of Chemistry* by Harry B. Gray and Gilbert P. Haight and would appreciate receiving any information that would enable us to do so.

To the Teacher

This book instructs students in writing the kind of expository prose that is required in short essay answers to exam questions, and it exemplifies methods of paragraph and essay development often used in longer papers in university course work. But more than anything else, it demonstrates to the student that he has experiences in life that are legitimate topics for discussion and exposition.

The teacher should attempt to relate composition, and the methods of development stressed in the book, to the way students must perform in other courses in their academic curriculum. It would be extremely helpful to students if, for example, teachers could get from lecturers in the university examples of questions typically asked on essay examinations. Even more beneficial would be samples of what the lecturers consider good answers. Such samples and consequent activities might begin after Chapter 2. Similar illustrative material on the term paper or critical essay might come after Chapter 3. In addition to the quality of ideas expressed, most university lecturers look for their clear expression and orderly arrangements. If the student can see that what he does in the composition course will help him to meet the expectations of his lecturers throughout the university, this will be one of the greatest motivational factors in the writing course. Along with the exercises in this book, and other activities as well, the teacher could therefore call attention to the academic rewards that may come to the student who writes well.

We do not mean to imply that success in the university is the final goal. Quite the contrary. The ability to consciously shape one's language, whether written or spoken, gives one a power over one's destiny that no other skill can match. With adequate language skills one can enter into interior dialogue with oneself to reinforce or redirect one's own being, and one can thus often influence the thoughts and behaviour of others. This distinctly human characteristic enables mankind to exercise personal and social capabilities far exceeding the expectations of its artless origins.

Any instructional device is only as successful as the teacher who uses it. This material is very dependent on the experiences and attitude the teacher brings, and the ingenuity and empathy with which he approaches students. Realising that other instructional activities in addition to the book will be used in the classroom, we hope that a spirit of co-operative effort and sharing between class and teacher can encourage confidence among students. A workshop atmosphere is desirable, wherein discussion about the model paragraphs and essays leads to the primary focus of the book, which is an understanding of the techniques employed in writing about these subjects, and where answers to exercises are developed co-operatively, with writing practice being evaluated through group effort and individual self-criticism.

Sentence-Writing Processes

Students in the course for which you have selected this textbook are no doubt still plagued with sentence-level writing decisions and problems. Students may make sentence-level 'errors.' Because of restricted or ineffective training in writing academic prose, students are often immature or unsophisticated writers, relying on simple prose styles inappropriate in the university. They may still have only a tenuous control of the mechanics of written English, including spelling and punctuation.

This composition book gives little attention to sentence-level difficulties, for we feel that exercises and activities at the sentence-level, as appropriate as they are, do not mix well with the paragraph and essay-level activities presented in this text. Grammar, spelling and punctuation, and other sentence-level problems can and should receive necessary attention between the lessons presented in this text. Preferably, such attention would come between methods of development rather than in the midst of a lesson in the book. This attention could be closely related to the homework assignments which appear at the end of each chapter.

Unremitting attention to sentence errors leaves the student little time for the more creative aspects of composition that are likely to lead to individual growth. We recommend a positive developmental approach to sentence revision. An understanding of sentence-writing processes does provide a base for developing mature writing. In the simplest terms, this understanding would include: (1) constituents that make up a complete sentence, (2) modification, (3) sentence expansion through addition, co-ordination, and embedding, and (4) transition between sentences. Transitional devices are discussed in the text.

Vocabulary

One of the important marks of a good writer is the effective use of an expanding vocabulary. Yet vocabulary development is one of the most elusive aspects of the composition class. It is often relegated to the reading portion of the student's English class; or it is assumed that the student will acquire the necessary vocabulary through other course work. Sometimes it is totally ignored as an unmanageable task.

Many students fail, however, in university reading and writing tasks through an inadequate or underdeveloped vocabulary. In this book we have given attention to some one hundred words and concepts. We have selected items on the basis of two criteria: those we anticipate may cause some confusion for many students, and those that illustrate a technique of vocabulary expansion. There are doubtless many additional vocabulary items which will require attention in your classroom. Such words can easily be identified by the teacher who has intimate knowledge of his students. The underlying principle behind vocabulary study should be the adequate contextualisation of the concept, so that students may perceive the relationship between meaning and form. Grammatical and situational (or semantic) contexts must be adequate to enable students to understand words. Dictionary work obviously helps, but it is the understanding of the communicative function of the words in a written context that leads to vocabulary growth.

The Textbook and the Classroom

The book provides for a great deal of individualised learning. The sequencing of the materials is carefully designed and has been tried out in the classroom, and, hopefully, the directions and explanations are clear, so that students will experience a minimum of difficulty in following them, leaving the teacher free to give guidance where it is needed.

Each lesson in the text should be approached with the view, conveyed to the class, that mastery of this lesson will have a direct influence on the students' performance in other academic work. Specific examples—of how the methods of development demonstrated and practised in the textbook relate to the students' activities in their other classes—are not spelled out in the book, because the situations in which it will be used are so varied. It is the teacher's responsibility to provide such specific instances for students. For instance, it should be easy enough to demonstrate how the simple list paragraph, the first studied in this book, can serve as a good answer in an essay examination.

In most situations, students will probably not be expected to cover any of the material at home beyond the specific homework assignments at the end of each chapter. Most students will be able to approach these homework assignments with confidence, only if the materials and exercises have received explicit attention during the class periods. A workshop atmosphere, where this is possible, with the teacher acting as a discussion leader and resource person during the actual writing process, can develop a comfortable writing environment, providing maximum support for the students' efforts. This is totally unlike the typical home or hostel environment, in which the student usually works alone, and is unaided by the stimulation of discussion, advice, or outside resources.

The textbook is not designed to provide the entire experience for a composition class. In some situations, it might provide up to half of the class work; in others, it might provide less. Although it is extremely hazardous to predict the amount of time required to master the materials, we can say that many of the lessons can be completed in one period, with homework and its discussion intervening between lessons. You will note throughout the book, however, that certain lessons are a great deal more complex and would require several periods for their completion. The only guidance we suggest is that classes should not spend so much time on a lesson that it becomes tedious for the students, but that they should spend enough time to be able to approach the homework with confidence and to be able to achieve reasonable success with the assignments.

Generally a three-step process in teaching the model paragraph and its exercises is effective in the classroom: (1) silent reading of the model paragraph, (2) discussion of the subject matter, and (3) doing the exercises.

Students should be encouraged to read each paragraph silently and carefully, with attention primarily on the method of development. Some guidance is given in the book prior to the model paragraphs, to suggest points to keep in mind while reading. Typical students will be more interested, in the first reading at least, in the subject matter and will read for the sense or meaning of the paragraph. We certainly do not wish to discourage this. Model paragraphs have been especially written to appeal to student interests, but the primary aim of the models is to illustrate the methods of development of expository prose. Doubtless, most students will need to read the models a second time to give fuller attention to the organisation of the paragraph.

Step two should capitalise on the students' interest in the subject matter. Class discussion on the content along with developmental vocabulary work is certainly an appropriate means to understanding the communicative function of contemporary prose. The teacher's role in these discussions should be one of summarising, emphasising important points in the discussion, relating the discussion directly to the model, and calling attention to the stated facts or opinions of the model when emotions carry the class beyond these facts. Whatever the discussion of the subject matter involves, the teacher should lead the class rather quickly to step three. In some lessons, the teacher will wish to conduct steps two and three simultaneously.

The major emphasis in the class period should be on the exercises. Some exercises can be done through class discussion, but others require individual pencil-and-paper work. All exercises should be discussed and answers mutually agreed on, before further model paragraphs are attempted. During the written work in class, the teacher should move around the room, checking over the students' work, correcting false starts, suggesting directions or points for the students to consider, and noting special difficulties which might be discussed with the class as a whole.

Homework

The completion of homework assignments is extremely important for the success of these materials. They provide the student with an opportunity for extended, thoughtful attention to a writing problem, to which he applies the developmental methods presented in each chapter.

It is essential that homework compositions be corrected, returned promptly, and thoroughly discussed before going to the next method of development. Since this book will probably not be the only resource for your course, other activities might intervene between chapters while you catch up with paper work. The correction of the compositions will reveal difficulties which the students are having, and these will influence your plan of operation for subsequent activities. It is possible, for example, that certain groups of students may require more writing practice than is provided in the book. Some students may need more sentence-level work. Still others may require a slower pace and more thorough discussion of their own writing before new material is introduced.

Homework assignments turned in by students can be valuable teaching aids. Student compositions, both good and bad, (projected with an opaque projector, for instance) can be used with the entire class, to illustrate alternatives selected by individual student writers. It is especially helpful, if students are writing about the same subject but with some freedom of choice in the content, to see the various strategies, decisions, and choices of others. Students can then develop a critical sense of writing, arriving at judgements about the merits of one choice over another in respect to sentence structure, word choice, transitional devices, method of development in relation to subject matter, overall effectiveness, and so on. Student compositions are likely to strike them as interesting and relevant, and are likely to motivate them more than the tired prose found in some of their regular textbooks. More importantly, student compositions present writing at a level with which the class is comfortable, a level which is a step in their progress toward the writing goals illustrated by the model paragraphs in this book.

To the Student

In some parts of the world, people have lost reverence for the printed page and have gained an independence from it through the increasing availability of such non-print media as recordings, films, radio, television, and audio and video cassettes. However, despite electronic advances in the communications field, reading is still very much a key to your success in acquiring the information and knowledge essential to formal education, and writing is still the primary tool for recording and organising your knowledge into useful and reusable notes. Writing may also be important for you to demonstrate to your teachers that you have acquired the information and skills necessary to join the ranks of the educated. In the general world of work and pleasure, you may not be asked to do much formal 'writing,' but you will be surrounded and sometimes victimised by other people's writing all your life. In both secondary school and university the art of writing (or composition as it is traditionally called) is one aspect of academic success over which you have a great deal of control. You should take the opportunity to master it now.

The purpose of this textbook is to help you gain confidence and skill in writing university-level compositions. A *composition* is any organised, self-contained piece of writing written—or 'composed'—for a special purpose, often an assignment in class. The term is frequently used for writing assignments in an English or composition class, where it usually means a self-conscious process in which you may make thoughtful decisions concerning what to say, how to organise and develop your ideas, and what words to use.

Writing a good composition requires the mastery of several skills. It requires grammatical accuracy and acceptability, so that relationships between words are clear, and understanding between reader and writer is made easier. It requires that the mechanics of punctuation, capitalisation, spelling, footnoting, perhaps even handwriting follow acceptable conventions. Additionally, it requires vocabulary appropriate to the subject matter and to the level and tone of writing. Finally, writing a good composition requires a careful and planned structuring of ideas. It is this skill—the structuring of ideas—which receives attention in this book. The book is not intended to teach you everything you need to know to be a better writer, but it should be an important part of your resources for writing improvement.

In some classes, personal feelings and self-expression in writing may be rewarded; but most teachers require proof that you know the facts. Your understanding of these facts is most commonly presented through educated prose—structured, disciplined, thoughtful composition. We feel we can best show how ideas are structured by directing your attention to the techniques of writing paragraphs. This book therefore focuses on the organisational foundation of all expository writing, the paragraph. Essays, or longer compositions, are treated as extensions of the techniques shown in writing paragraphs, which may be about people, events, or ideas.

Let us explain next how we hope to accomplish our aim of enabling you to write better paragraphs. Specifically, each lesson in the book gives you a number of model paragraphs to read and study. The paragraphs in one lesson demonstrate or exemplify one technique of paragraph development. Exercises that closely follow the organisation of the model paragraphs provide you with an *analysis* of the particular paragraph's structure; this should be a basis for a general *understanding* of paragraph development. This general understanding is then employed in additional exercises and homework assignments that require *practice* of the writing techniques illustrated in the lesson. The lessons foster a sense of progress because each one enables you to master a specific technique or skill before you embark on the next one. Every third lesson in the text extends the techniques learned to the writing of an essay or long paper.

It may appear in individual lessons that we encourage practice of a certain type of paragraph development for its own sake. This is not the case. We have tried to select only a few of the most useful types of paragraph organisation, but they are useful only if they satisfy the organisational requirements of your particular writing task. The writing practice is intended to build up a repertoire of several different types of paragraph development which, with increasing ease, you can select and use effectively in your own writing assignments. In Chapter 15 and elsewhere, we show that we have not simply made up these paragraph types, but rather that they appear with frequency in the formal writings of others. The ultimate goal we see for you is that you will be able to approach any subject, feeling confident that you can develop and express your ideas on that subject through the methods discussed in this book.

The general subject matter of this book is, of course, writing—a subject about which you may or may not share our enthusiasm. In either case, we have tried to make the particular subject matter of the model paragraphs reflect matters of general interest. Some topics for model paragraphs were chosen because they are typical of the writing assignments in history, psychology, sociology, economics, and so on. Other topics were chosen because they help demonstrate the techniques of paragraph development which we feel are most productive. But all were chosen because we consider them legitimate classroom topics which are frequently ignored in traditional composition texts. We have deliberately included material on educational alternatives, university examinations, how to succeed in an interview, on art, sports, film criticism, social change, and on the economic requirements of modernising nations. A major goal of this book, then, is to demonstrate that formal methods of organising ideas will facilitate communication regardless of the topics discussed.

We believe there are a few techniques of paragraph development that can be learned easily if they are clearly presented and carefully practiced. The understanding and practice of these techniques should have the immediate result of enabling you to write simply and effectively about a variety of topics on which you already have ideas. It should also encourage you to continue the conscious study of the ways in which ideas are organised and expressed in the writings of others. We further believe that the mastery of these techniques will assure success in this course and most certainly increase the prospect of success in any course requiring a substantial amount of writing.

1
Paragraph development by listing

1.1   Read the model paragraph. As you read, pay close attention to both the meaning and the organisation of the ideas discussed.

Sentence Functions in Paragraph Development

The *sentences in* most well written *paragraphs* may be analysed into *four* general *functions*. First, there are paragraph *introducers,* which are sentences that *establish* the *topic focus* of the paragraph as a whole. Second, there are paragraph *developers,* which *present* examples or *details* of various kinds that support the ideas set forth by the paragraph introducers. Third, there are viewpoint or context *modulators,* which are sentences that *provide* a smooth *transition* between different sets of ideas. Fourth, there are paragraph *terminators,* which logically *conclude* the *ideas* discussed in the paragraph in a psychologically satisfying manner. Not all pieces of writing will conform to this analysis; however, most successful *paragraphs* usually contain some combination of these *four sentence types*.

1.1a   Each sentence in the paragraph contains a key idea. The key idea can be expressed in a short phrase often using key words appearing in the sentence. The key words that form the key ideas in each sentence of the model paragraph are in italics. From each of the six sentences, write the italicised words on the following lines.

1
2
3
4
5
6

1.1b   What function do paragraph developers serve? Identify the four paragraph developers used in the model paragraph.

1.1c   What function do context modulators serve? Do they appear in every well written paragraph? Does this paragraph contain a context modulator?

1.1d   Is the final sentence in the model paragraph a good terminator? That is, does it end the paragraph by bringing it to a psychologically satisfying conclusion?

1.1e The type of paragraph presented on page 1 is called a list paragraph. To avoid a 'shopping list' appearance, certain words or phrases are used to help the paragraph proceed smoothly. Point out the words or devices that are employed to aid the listing of details.

1.2 Read the model paragraph. This time, as you read try to observe three main parts of paragraph organisation.

Black African Nations

During the decade of the 1960's, most of the European colonies of Sub-Saharan Africa achieved independence. In the west, Nigeria (1960), Sierra Leone (1961), and Gambia (1965)—all former British colonies—joined the family of free and independent nations. In the east, Tanzania (1961), Uganda (1962), Kenya (1963), and Zambia (1964) also became sovereign states free of British rule. As the African empire of Great Britain was being dismantled, France, the other major European coloniser, withdrew from vast areas south of the Sahara. Thirteen former French colonies gained national status in the single year 1960: Mauritania, Senegal, Mali, Ivory Coast, Upper Volta, Togo, Dahomey, Niger, Chad, Central African Republic, Cameroon, Gabon, and Congo. Although a few European colonialists still occupy African territory, the 1960's witnessed the birth of more than twenty free, black nations.

1.2a Does this paragraph contain the essential elements of a well written paragraph—introducer, developers, terminator? Point out the sentence or sentences that serve as the introducer, the developers, the terminator.

1.2b In addition to the three types of sentences mentioned in the previous question, this paragraph contains a viewpoint or context modulator. That is, a sentence that provides a transition between different sets of ideas. Identify the sentence that performs this transition function.

1.2c Review (see sentence 5 of paragraph 1.1 and exercise 1.1d) the function of a paragraph terminator. Is the final sentence of 1.2 an adequate terminator?

1.3 The following list paragraph gives information about several island nations. How many of these nations are familiar to you?

Island Nations

Many Americans and Europeans are accustomed to thinking of a *country* only as a governmental unit that occupies part of a large continent, but the fact is that there are some very important countries—especially in Asian Pacific waters—that are composed entirely of widely scattered islands. As a first example, the Republic of the Philippines has a gross national product (GNP)[1] of over $4,856,000,000 and a population of 37,008,419 inhabitants, spread over approximately 3000 islands, the largest of which are Luzon, Mindanao, and Samar._____

_____

_____

On the basis of these three instances (and others could be mentioned such as New Zealand, Sri Lanka (formerly Ceylon), and Singapore), it may be concluded that some of the island nations of South-East Asia are among the more prominent governments in international affairs.

1.3a Does the paragraph meet the requirements of a list paragraph? What is missing from the paragraph?

1.3b Finish the paragraph by writing in the space provided two developers, one about Indonesia and one about Japan. In the table below is some information that you may want to use. Begin your sentence about Indonesia with *Secondly;* your sentence about Japan with *Thirdly.*

COUNTRY	GNP	POPULATION	NO. OF ISLANDS
Indonesia	$11,100,000,000	122,864,000 (1971 est.)	3,000 approximately Large islands include: Java, Sumatra, Kalimantan, Sulawesi, West Irian.
Japan	$124,700,000,000	104,649,000 (1970)	1,000 approximately Four major islands: Honshu, Kyushu, Hokkaido, Shikoku.

1.4 Read the model paragraph. This time as you read, try to observe three main parts of paragraph organisation.

Cooking Methods and Some English Colloquialisms

Basic methods of preparing food show great similarity throughout the world, but English cooking terms sometimes have

[1] Gross National Product is the total monetary value of all goods and services produced in a given period of time.

special meanings. For example, almost all cultures have devised some means of baking, that is cooking bread or other food in an oven. Boiling, or cooking food in water or some other liquid, is another universal practice. A related process, stewing, means to boil slowly or gently a mixture usually of meat, vegetables, and water. Still another cooking process, roasting, means to cook meat in its own juices over an open fire or in an oven. While the terms to describe the various cooking methods have a literal meaning in formal English, in informal English they are sometimes used to describe human behaviour in a colourful or humorous way. *Half-baked,* for instance, may refer to a foolish idea or a stupid person. *Boiling* or *boiling mad* means very angry. *In a stew* means to be worried or to be in a difficult situation, and to *stew in one's own juices* means to suffer, especially from one's own actions. To *roast* a person means to criticise or ridicule him without mercy. In other cases, a person, through his excessive *relish* of life, might get *pickled* and end up *in a jam.* This brief list demonstrates the use of cooking terms as colloquial expressions to picture human conduct more vividly.

1.4a What is the name and function of the first sentence in the model paragraph of 1.4?

1.4b What is the name and function of sentences 2 to 5 in the paragraph?

1.4c This paragraph contains a viewpoint or context modulator, that is, a transition sentence. Remember that this is a sentence that provides a transition between different sets of ideas. Identify the sentence that performs this transition function. What two sets of ideas does it connect?

1.4d In the model paragraph of 1.1, transitional words such as *first* and *second* are used in the development of the paragraph. Find transitional words in paragraph 1.4. For each, explain how it relates one idea to another.

1.4e What is the name and function of the final sentence?

1.5 As you read the next paragraph, try to make an objective evaluation of yourself in relation to the points mentioned.

Looking forward to the decade of the 1980's, one wonders what personal qualities will be needed for success. Possibly the four most essential attributes are flexibility, honesty, creativity, and perseverance. First, our rapidly changing society requires flexibility—the ability to adapt oneself readily to new ideas and experiences. Next, honesty, the capacity both to tell and to face the truth courageously, will be important in all aspects of personal and public relations._____

_____

_____

_____

Just as these attributes of character are desirable today, so in the future they will surely continue to be decisive in determining personal success.

1.5a Although this is also a list paragraph, it differs slightly in form from the previous ones. Notice that there are two sentences that function as paragraph introducers. The first is a topic introducer, which establishes the topic discussion—personal qualities for success. The second sentence, the topic sentence, more narrowly defines or delimits the topic. In this case, we know that the discussion will be limited to four attributes—flexibility, honesty, creativity, perseverance. Think about the importance of the personal qualities of *creativity* and *perseverance*. Write two additional sentences in the blanks provided which develop the discussion of these two qualities. You will need to use connectors, or transition words, to relate your sentences to the previous developers.

1.5b Write a title in the blank space provided directly above the paragraph. Look at the titles of other paragraphs in the lesson. The first word and all important words in a title should be capitalised. Notice that a good title is brief and gives some indication of the content or point of view of the paragraph. The topic introducer and the topic sentence provide the necessary information for you to write a good title.

1.5c Discuss with your teacher and fellow students the concepts of flexibility, honesty, creativity, and perseverance. Name some famous people or personal acquaintances who possess these qualities.

1.6 Remember that a list paragraph has several parts. First, paragraph introducers—both a topic introducer and a topic sentence or just a topic sentence—are used to open a paragraph. Next, supporting examples are listed with the aid of connectors. Sometimes transition or modulator sentences are used between different sets of ideas. Finally, a terminator sentence brings the paragraph to a logical conclusion.

With these ideas in mind, write your own list paragraph. Give your paragraph a title. You may choose one of the topics given below.

Internationally known artists (or musicians or actors or writers)

Important national or regional handicrafts

Qualities of a good teacher (or leader or friend)

Athletes from a particular continent or block in the last Olympic Games

Topic of your choice

2
Paragraph development by examples

2.1 This lesson is concerned with the use of examples in the development of paragraphs. The example paragraph is a kind of list paragraph, in which example sentences closely support the topic sentence. There is, of course, a terminator. Examine the following paragraph.

Effective Writing—A Must in Universities

The *ability to write* well organised, concise paragraphs is *essential* to a student's success in almost all university courses. In preparing scientific *reports* of laboratory experiments, a student must present his findings in *logical order* and *clear language* in order to receive a favourable evaluation of his work. To write successful answers to essay questions on history or anthropology examinations, a student must arrange the relevant facts and opinions according to some accepted pattern of paragraph structure. And certainly when a student writes a book report for English, or a critique for political studies, or a term paper for sociology, style and organisation are often as important as content. Clearly, skill in expository writing is crucial to successful achievement in most university subjects.

2.1a The key words or ideas in the first two sentences of the paragraph are in italics. Write these words on the first two lines below. Find the key ideas in the remaining sentences and write short phrases for each on lines 3 to 5. In writing the short phrases, you may use words of your own or those in the sentences.

1
2
3
4
5

2.1b Familiarise yourself with the following symbols and definitions which will be used in analysing paragraph structure:

TS —stands for topic sentence, a sentence that states the main idea of a paragraph.

E —stands for example sentence, a sentence that presents a specific example or illustration related to the topic sentence.

R —stands for restatement sentence, a sentence that in essence repeats or restates the main idea of the topic sentence in different words. The restatement gives the effect of rounding off the paragraph by circling back to the idea of the topic sentence. The restatement is one kind of paragraph terminator.

2.1c Which sentence in the model paragraph of 2.1 expresses the main idea of the paragraph? Remember that the sentence which expresses the main idea of a paragraph is called the topic sentence (TS).

2.1d What is the relationship between sentence 2 and sentence 1? Which sentence expresses a general idea? Which sentence (E) presents a specific example?

2.1e What is the relationship between sentence 3 and sentence 1? What is the relationship between sentence 3 and sentence 2?

2.1f Does the final sentence function as an adequate terminator? Why?

2.1g The following symbols describe the structure of paragraph 2.1. TS / E1, E2, E3 / R

2.2 The sentences listed below are not arranged in the logical paragraph sequence of topic sentence, examples, and restatement. Study the list carefully and try to decide which sentence makes a general statement, which sentences present illustrations, and which sentence repeats the idea of the general statement. Write a number before each sentence to show its logical position in a well ordered paragraph.

___

__Clearly, in agriculture and in industry, the progress of a country depends on the busy hands of its working people.

__Finally, the establishment of efficient transportation and communication systems, essential services in a modernising economy, relies heavily on a labour force of expert craftsmen who take pride in their manual skills.

__And of course the manufacture as well as the maintenance of machines of all kinds demands a large number of trained mechanics and technicians.

__To begin with, ploughing fields, planting and harvesting crops, and raising livestock are all important to development and all require people who work with their hands.

__Secondly, mining natural resources, building roads and bridges, and constructing dams for irrigation and electrical power are also important to development and also require people who know how to use their hands skilfully.

__Manual labour is one of the principal development resources in any industralising country, as the following examples demonstrate.

2.2a Read the sentences in the arrangement you have established in order to experience the paragraph as a unified whole.

2.2b What symbols would you use to describe the paragraph structure? _____

2.2c Examine closely the sentence which you selected for the topic sentence. How do the ideas of this sentence relate to the ideas of the four example sentences?

2.2d In terms of ideas, what do the topic sentence and the restatement sentence have in common?

2.2e There are four developers—example sentences—in this paragraph. Give reasons for arranging these in the sequence you used.

2.2f Write a title for the paragraph in the space provided. Recall that a good title should be short and should tell the reader what the paragraph is about.

2.3 In the following paragraph two elements are missing—a topic sentence and a restatement sentence. As you read the example sentences try to think of a TS and an R which might begin and end the paragraph.

Social Concerns in Modern Literature

_____

_____

For example, many contemporary novels of Africa and India depict the lives of ordinary people struggling against adversity. Furthermore, poetry from South America and North America speaks out against social and economic oppression. In still another instance, modern European drama enacts the fate of the working man in his drab confrontation with life. Even films, popular songs, and folk drama from all around the world, tell the story of the little man and his battle against the giants of impersonal corporations, remote governments, or aggressive neighbouring nations. _____

_____

_____

2.3a In the space at the beginning of the paragraph write a topic sentence. The sentence should be a general statement that would cause a reader to want more information in the form of specific examples.

2.3b At the end of the paragraph write a restatement sentence. This sentence should do two things: (1) repeat or restate in different words the ideas of the topic sentence; (2) terminate the listing of examples so that the reader feels that a satisfactory conclusion has been reached.

2.3c What symbols would you use to describe the structure of this paragraph?_____

2.3d Learn to spell, pronounce, and use all unfamiliar words in the paragraph.

2.4 In the following paragraph two elements are missing—a topic sentence and a restatement sentence. As you read the example sentences try to think of a TS and an R which might begin and end the paragraph.

_____

_____

_____

_____

For example, in the less populated regions of the world such as tribal areas, laws or customs may be enforced by a council of elders or by a strong chief or leader of the tribe much in the manner of a father who decides what behaviour is best for his children. As another example, in the sparsely populated great open land of places like Australia, Canada, Siberia, and Brazil, a few policemen must travel great distances to enforce laws made to protect people and property. In countries where most of the people live in crowded urban areas, on the other hand, law enforcement is usually in the hands of large numbers of police who are directly responsible to the chief governmental official for that area. As still another instance, countries have cooperated in establishing various organisations and methods, including military or police action, to enforce the rules and laws agreed to by a majority of the co-operating nations._____

2.4a In the space at the beginning of the paragraph write a topic sentence. The sentence should be a general statement that would cause a reader to want more information in the form of specific examples.

2.4b At the end of the paragraph write a restatement sentence. This sentence should do two things: (1) repeat or restate in different words the ideas of the topic sentences; (2) terminate the listing of examples so that the reader feels that a satisfactory conclusion has been reached.

2.4c Write a title in the blank space provided directly above the paragraph.

2.4d Using symbols, what is the structure of the resulting paragraph?

_____

2.5 As you read the next paragraph, observe the transitional devices used to move from one example to another.

In the United States any person who completes elementary and secondary school (grades 1 to 12) has a variety of advanced educational opportunities from which to choose. For those people interested in a four year general education in preparation for work or further university study in such professional schools as law, medicine, or dentistry, there are hundreds of liberal arts colleges throughout the country with widely varying curricula. For those who want a four year technical education in one of the arts or sciences, there are specialised schools in, for example, music or engineering or architecture. For the person who wants to enter the labour force in a particular vocation and with modest preparation in general education, most states and cities provide two year community colleges. Increasingly important in recent years are technical institutes sponsored by various businesses and industries solely for the training of their own employees. This brief summary of educational opportunities available to high school graduates in the United States suggests that organised learning can continue for several years beyond the basic twelve grades.

2.5a   Using symbols, what is the structure of the paragraph?_____

_____

2.5b   Review exercises 1.1a and 2.1a. In these exercises you made outlines of the model paragraphs. This is a good way to take notes on anything you read. Making an outline is also a good way to organise your thoughts when preparing to write a paragraph or an essay. Find the key ideas in each sentence of paragraph 2.5 and write short phrases for each on the lines below.

_____   1
_____   2
_____   3
_____   4
_____   5
_____   6

2.6   Think about the educational alternatives within your country. Write a paragraph about educational alternatives in your country for people who have completed their basic education. The paragraph should contain six sentences: a topic sentence, four developers, and a restatement. The topic sentence might begin with the words *In my country* . . . . The first developer might begin with the words *For those people interested in a general education* . . . . The second developer might begin with the words *For those who want a technical education* . . . .

3
Essay
development by
examples

3.1 Read the model paragraph.

The Successful Interview

¹To be successful in a job interview (or for that matter in almost
any interview situation), the applicant should demonstrate
certain personal and professional qualities. ²In as much as the
first and often lasting impression of a person is determined by
the clothes he wears, the job applicant should take care to
appear well-groomed and modestly dressed, avoiding the extremes of too elaborate or too casual attire. ³Besides care for
personal appearance, he should pay close attention to his manner
of speaking, which should be neither ostentatious nor familiar
but rather straightforward, grammatically accurate, and friendly.
⁴In addition, he should be prepared to talk knowledgeably
about the requirements of the position for which he is applying
in relation to his own professional experience and interests.
⁵And finally, the really impressive applicant must convey a
sense of self-confidence and enthusiasm for work, factors which
all interviewers value highly. ⁶The job seeker who displays
these characteristics, with just a little luck, will certainly succeed
in the typical personnel interview.

3.1a Using the symbols that were introduced in lesson two (2.1b)
to describe the functional relationship of sentences in a paragraph,
assign an appropriate symbol to each sentence in this paragraph.

Sentence 1_____ Sentence 4_____
Sentence 2_____ Sentence 5_____
Sentence 3_____ Sentence 6_____

3.1b What is the function of sentence 1? What role does it play in
the paragraph?

3.1c What contribution to the development of the paragraph do
sentences 2, 3, 4, and 5 make?

3.1d Is sentence 6 necessary to the structure of a well written paragraph? If so, why? If not, why not?

3.1e Discuss in class the meanings of
person   *personal*   *personnel*

knowledge	*knowledgeable*	*knowledgeably*
succeed	*success*	*successful*
ostentatious		

3.1f   Find the key ideas in each of the sentences of the paragraph and write short phrases for each on the lines below. You may use words from the sentences or words of your own to express the key ideas.

Successful interview requires certain qualities _____ 1

_____ 2

_____ 3

_____ 4

_____ 5

_____ 6

3.2   In the previous exercise (3.1a) the symbols that describe the organisation of the model paragraph were indicated.

TS / E1, E2, E3, E4 / R

The plan of the paragraph is very simple; it consists of only three parts:

   1 a topic sentence that presents a one-sentence statement of the main idea of the whole paragraph
   2 several example sentences that give details to support the main idea of the topic sentence
   3 a restatement sentence that reaffirms the central idea of the topic sentence.

   The basic TS / E.../ R paragraph plan can be extended to provide the plan for an essay also consisting of three parts:

   1 a topic paragraph (TP) that introduces the main idea of the whole essay
   2 one or more example paragraphs (EP), each one of which presents a main point with its supporting details
   3 a restatement paragraph (RP) that once again focuses attention on the main idea of the topic paragraph.

As you read the following essay, try to observe its plan of organisation.

The Successful Interview

___To be successful in a job interview (or for that matter in almost any interview situation), you should demonstrate certain personal and professional qualities. You need to create a good image in the limited time available, usually from 30 to 45 minutes. Furthermore, you must make a positive impression which the interviewer will remember while he interviews other applicants. At all times, you should present your most attractive qualities during an interview.

___ You should, for example, take care to appear well-groomed and modestly dressed, avoiding the extremes of too elaborate or too casual attire. On the positive side, clothes may be a good leveller, putting you on a par with other applicants and requiring the interviewer to consider more important qualifications. On the other hand, clothes which are too informal may convey the impression that you are not serious about the job or that you may be casual about your work as well as your dress. Clothes which are too elaborate, too colourful, or too expensive suggest that you do not understand what behaviour is appropriate for the job or that you are snobbish or frivolous. The right clothes worn at the right time, however, gain the respect of the interviewer and his confidence in your judgement. It may not be true that 'clothes make the man,' but the first and often lasting impression of you is determined by the clothes you wear.

___ Besides care for personal appearance, you should pay close attention to your manner of speaking. Since speech is a reflection of personality, you should reflect confidence by speaking in a clear voice, loud enough to be heard without being aggressive or overpowering. Your speech should not call attention to itself, but it should reveal the individuality and ability of the speaker. Obviously, you must speak without grammatical or dialect differences for which you might be criticised or which might cause embarrassment to the employer. Although there are cultural differences with respect to the formality of the job interview, your speech must show you to be a friendly and pleasant person.

___ Speaking without a subject worth talking about will not impress anyone. You should be prepared to talk knowledgeably about the requirements of the position for which you are applying in relation to your own professional experiences and interests. Knowing something about the position enables you to ask intelligent questions about the work and the requirements for the job. The interviewer can decide from the questions asked whether you are genuinely interested or knowledgeable. You can comment on your own training, experience, and other qualifications in relation to the specific tasks of the position. The interviewer can determine whether your background and potential seem to fit the position. The position for which you are applying is not only the safest topic for discussion, it is essential that you demonstrate your understanding of the requirements and your abilities in meeting these requirements.

___ Finally, to be really impressive you must convey a sense of self-confidence and enthusiasm for work. As already indicated, you demonstrate self-confidence by your manner of speech and dress. You further show it by being prepared for the interview with information and questions about the position. In addition, the way you enter the room, sit, look at the interviewer, and fill out application forms and other papers may express self-confidence. The eagerness with which you discuss the job rather than the salary may reveal your enthusiasm for work. You may express it also through your questions and comments about working conditions and facilities. And, of course, your previous experience and success will tell the interviewer about your enthusiasm for work. Both of these qualities—self-confidence and enthusiasm for work—are valued highly by all interviewers.

___   The appropriately dressed job applicant indicates his sound judgement. His manner of speaking suggests his friendliness and competence. His curiosity and information about the position he is seeking demonstrate his sincerity and potential in the job. He exhibits self-confidence through his knowledge, and he shows his enthusiasm for work. If you display these characteristics, with just a little luck, you will certainly succeed in the typical personnel interview.

3.2a Label each paragraph in the model essay using the symbols TP (for topic paragraph), EP (for example paragraph), and RP (for restatement paragraph). Since there are several EP's, number them consecutively EP1, EP2, EP3, and so on.

3.2b Underline the topic sentence in the TP. Does this sentence also state the main idea of the whole essay?

3.2c Underline the sentence that states the main point in EP1. Does the main point of this paragraph come first in the paragraph?

3.2d What relationship do the unmarked sentences in EP1 have to the underlined sentence?

3.2e Underline the sentence that states the main point in EP2, in EP3, and in EP4. Do the main points of these paragraphs come first?

3.2f What relationship do the unmarked sentences in each example paragraph have to the underlined sentence in that paragraph?

3.2g Underline the restatement sentence in the RP. Does it come first in the paragraph? What relationship does it have to the unmarked sentences in this paragraph? Does the restatement sentence also round off the whole theme by referring back to the topic paragraph? If so, how?

3.2h Notice that the model paragraph 3.1 uses 'the applicant,' 'he,' 'the job applicant,' and 'the job seeker' as subjects of the sentences. The model essay 3.2, however, uses 'you' as the subject of most sentences. What is the effect of this change?

Notice also that the final paragraph of the model essay starts with 'the job applicant' as subject and continues with 'he' as the subject until the final sentence. What is the effect of this? Why is 'the job applicant' used as subject in the final paragraph? Why does the final sentence return to 'you' as subject?

3.2i Transitional words or phrases are important in writing an essay. They help connect and show the relationship of the various parts, or paragraphs, of the essay.

Study the following section on the various transitional devices used. Notice how the transitional words or phrases move the reader from one topic to another, from one point of view to another, or from one example to another.

PARAGRAPH	TRANSITION	RELATIONSHIP
TP	you...you	The most important way to show relationship between sentences is to use the same subject throughout a paragraph.
TP	Furthermore...	Indicates that an additional point will follow.
TP	At all times...	Moves the reader from specific ideas in sentences 2 and 3 to a general summary in sentence 4.
EP1	...for example...	Introduces the first example and relates EP1 to the TP.
EP1	On the positive side...	Indicates that a positive illustration of EP1 will follow.
EP1	On the other hand...	Indicates that another illustration of EP1—a contrasting illustration—will follow.
EP1	...however...	Changes the point of view from 'too casual,' 'too elaborate, too colourful too expensive' to 'the right clothes'.

Prepare a chart similar to the one above, listing transitional devices from EP2, EP3, EP4, and the RP. Say how the transitional words indicate the relationships between ideas in sentences or paragraphs.

3.2j Now read the model paragraph 3.1 again to discover the relationship between the paragraph and the essay. Notice in the essay that the sentences you have underlined are exactly like, or nearly like, the sentences in the model paragraph. The TS in the model paragraph had been expanded to become the TP in the essay. E1 becomes the topic sentence for EP1. E2 becomes the topic sentence for EP2, and so on. The R in the model paragraph, of course, becomes the topic sentence in the RP.

3.3 Write an essay of six paragraphs with the structure TP / EP1, EP2, EP3, EP4 / RP. Choose a topic in which you are interested. Before writing your essay make a short phrase outline of the key ideas you plan to cover. Use the following short phrase outline of the essay in exercise 3.2 as a model. Have your teacher approve your outline before you write the essay.

The Successful Interview ⎤
Important personal and professional qualities |
   A good image in a short time   **TP**
   A lasting impression |
   Attractive qualities ⎦

      Well-groomed and modestly dressed ⎤
         Not too elaborate |
         Not too casual   **EP1**
         Right clothes gain respect ⎦

      Manner of speaking ⎤
         Clear and loud enough |
         Without grammatical or dialect differences   **EP2**
         Friendly and pleasant ⎦

      Know something about the job ⎤
         Requirements for the position   **EP3**
         Experience and knowledge ⎦

      Self-confidence and enthusiasm ⎤
         Be prepared for the interview   **EP4**
         Show your interest in the job ⎦

Dress ⎤
Speech |
Sincerity   **RP**
Self-confidence |
Succeeding in the interview ⎦

4
Paragraph
development by
comparison

4.1 A comparison paragraph, as its name indicates, compares similar aspects or qualities of two subjects. In this lesson two procedures will be followed. In the first procedure, an example related to one subject—A—alternates with an example related to another subject—B. In the second procedure, all examples of subject A are listed together, followed by all examples of subject B.

As you have learned in previous lessons, a well organised paragraph consists of several types of sentences. We have discussed the function of the topic sentence (TS), the example sentence (E), and the restatement sentence (R). In writing comparison paragraphs, however, additional sentence types may be used. In many paragraphs, for example, a topic introducer (TI) is used. The topic sentence then states more specifically the basis of comparison. Example sentences are, of course, still used but in this lesson will be marked as A-E1, B-E1, A-E2, B-E2, and so on, depending upon which subject the sentence is illustrating. Transition sentences (Tr) may be used to change from one point of view to another, from one set of ideas to another, or from one subject to another.

From Paragraph to Essay

Despite their obvious differences in length, the paragraph and the essay are quite similar structurally. For example, the paragraph is introduced by either a topic sentence or a topic introducer followed by a topic sentence. In the essay, the first paragraph provides introductory material and establishes the topic focus. Next, the sentences in the body of a paragraph develop the topic sentence. Similarly, the body of an essay consists of a number of paragraphs that expand and support the ideas presented in the introductory paragraph. Finally, a terminator—whether a restatement, conclusion, or observation—ends the paragraph. The essay, too, has a device which brings its ideas to a logically and psychologically satisfying completion: the concluding paragraph. Although exceptions to these generalisations may be observed in modern creative writing, most well written expository paragraphs and essays are comparable in structure.

4.1a Does this paragraph include the necessary parts discussed—topic sentence, developers, terminator? Identify them.

4.1b Classify the paragraph developers according to subject A or subject B. Is there a logical alternative?

4.1c Point out transitional devices—either words or phrases—used in this paragraph.

4.1d Do you think the final sentence is an adequate terminator? Why?

4.2 Read the following paragraph and notice the relationship between the subject A examples and the subject B examples.

The folk sculpture of black Africa has influenced many modern artists. Perhaps the most striking example of this influence is to be found in the obvious relationship between the African primitive artists and that Spanish genius, Pablo Picasso. Characterised by a bulkiness of form, the sculptures of the Africans appear solid and heavy. The characteristics of clay and wood media and the simplicity of the artists' tools, coupled with an imaginative conception of reality, often result in an exaggeration of human features. Typically associated with such serious events as reproduction and death, these sculptures nevertheless exhibit to the beholder a light spirit and a sense of humour. Also stressing the themes of love and death, Picasso used fantastic and grotesque shapes and colours to portray both the beauty and cruelty of human existence. Faces look in two directions; bodies are 'all eyes' or 'all feet'. Seated figures take on the appearance of featureless boulders. Consciously or unconsciously, Picasso and the African artists distort their subjects in similar ways to present a more intense vision of man.

4.2a Identify the topic introducer (TI) and the topic sentence (TS). Explain their relationship.

4.2b What form does this comparison paragraph have? That is, does it alternate examples of subject A and subject B, or does it list all A examples together, followed by all B examples together?

4.2c The examples describing aspects of African sculpture and Picasso's work are similar.

```
AFRICAN   A-E1  'solid and heavy'  ←─────────────────────┐
          E2  'exaggeration of human features' ←───────┐ │
          E3  'serious events...light spirit' ←──────┐ │ │
PICASSO   B-E1  'beauty and cruelty of human existence'─┘ │ │
          E2  'all eyes' or 'all feet'──────────────────┘ │
          E3  'featureless boulders'────────────────────────┘
```

Notice that the first example under Picasso is similar to the last example under African sculpture. Linking these two examples together makes a smooth transition from subject A to subject B.

The paragraph structure would be represented as follows:

TI / TS / A-E1, E2, E3; B-E1, E2, E3 / R

4.2d Write a title for the paragraph.

4.3 The following paragraph has no terminator. As you read, try to keep the main idea of the paragraph in mind so that you can write an effective restatement sentence.

Post-war West Germany and Japan

The re-emergence of West Germany and Japan as major world powers is one of the most remarkable stories of national recovery in the post-war period. In 1945, West Germany was devastated by war and occupied by foreign troops. Similarly, Japan, West Germany's far eastern war-time ally, also suffered great destruction and then occupation by U.S. forces. Yet within a single generation, through hard work, industrial know-how, and the co-operative assistance of former enemy countries, West Germany has experienced rapid economic development, attaining a degree of affluence as early as the 1960's. Making maximum use of the same combination of human and natural resources, in similar fashion Japan quickly achieved the status of one of the most productive and prosperous nations in the east or the west. Another factor in West Germany's progress has been an extended period of stable government. Japan, too, has enjoyed the benefit of orderly popular government, under a new political system which eliminated the old imperial authority. West Germany's accomplishments have not been limited to economics or politics; her new cultural importance was symbolised by the Nobel prize literature award to Heinrich Böll in 1972. Japanese cultural prominence—from traditional Kabuki to the art of contemporary film making—has been universally recognised, including a Nobel prize literature award to Yasunari Kawabata in 1968. _____

_____

_____

4.3a What form does this comparison paragraph have? That is, does it alternate examples of subject A and subject B, or does it list all A examples together, followed by all B examples together?

4.3b Are both a topic introducer and a topic sentence used?

4.3c In the space provided, supply a terminator to close the paragraph logically.

4.4 Read the following paragraph. In addition to observing the structure of the paragraph, pay attention to the kind of vocabulary used in a discussion of religions.

Similarities in Christianity and Islam

Two of the major religions of the world are Christianity and Islam. Although seemingly different, the two faiths share several fundamental beliefs and practices. Both worship the same deity, whom the Christians term God and the Muslims call Allah. For knowledge of his faith and for inspiration, the Christian turns to his holy book, the Bible. The Muslim, too, has a holy book, the Koran, which guides his prayers and gives meaning to his life. The Ten Commandments and the Sermon on the Mount provide a code of ethics for the lives of all Christians. Similarly, all Muslims subscribe to the Hadith and the Five Pillars of Faith for daily guidance. Such basic similarities in code and conduct illustrate the shared heritage of Christianity and Islam.

4.4a Discuss the function of each sentence in the paragraph and assign to each an appropriate symbol: TI, TS, A-E..., Tr, R. (Exclude sentence number three. Notice that sentence number three is an example of two subjects compared in a single sentence. This is one way of writing comparisons, but it is not emphasised in this lesson. If the sentence were assigned a symbol, it would be labeled as AB.)

4.4b Identify the transitional words or devices used.

4.4c What parallels can you find between the words or phrases of the restatement sentence and those of the topic sentence?

4.4d What meanings do the following words have for you: *faith, inspiration, ethics, deity, code, heritage, fundamental*?

4.5 As you read the following paragraph, pay particular attention to the example sentences, which constitute the paragraph developers. The two groups of people discussed in the paragraph represent the movement of rural populations to urban centres which is taking place in many parts of the world. Without the skills necessary for easy adaptation to urban living, these groups find it difficult to settle to the kind of life which attracted them to the big cities in the first place.

Problems of New Immigrants to New York City

Over the past decade, Puerto Ricans from the island of Puerto Rico and blacks from the southern part of the United States have contributed the most significant immigration populations to the New York City area. Both groups come from similar backgrounds and follow similar patterns in trying to adapt to the complexities of city life. As U.S. citizens, Puerto Ricans have the freedom to move from Puerto Rico to any location within the United States. Also as citizens, they have the responsibility of serving in the U.S. armed forces. Set apart from the average New Yorker by physical appearance and language difference, Puerto Ricans are compelled to cluster in certain neighbourhoods and thus become ghetto inhabitants. The children often arrive educationally disadvantaged due to under-financed school systems on the island. The adults generally possess rural skills rather than urban skills. From the rural South, blacks also arrive in the New York City area with skills insufficient to compete in urban life. Their children similarly are educationally handicapped because of separate and inferior schooling. Frequently sharing the same ghettoes with Puerto Ricans, the Southern blacks, with their distinctive speech and obvious physical characteristics, often live together in neighbourhoods segregated from those of the white New Yorker. Although they have the rights and responsibilities of U.S. citizenship, including military service, Southern blacks, like Puerto Ricans, find it extremely difficult to achieve full citizenship in a hostile urban environment. Both of these groups share similar socio-economic characteristics and suffer similar problems of adjustment in a technologically oriented urban setting.

4.5a Classify the paragraph developers according to subject A or subject B.

4.5b What parallels can you find between the subject A examples and subject B examples? Notice that the first and second examples under subject A (As U.S. Citizens,...Also as citizens....) are compressed into a single example sentence under subject B (Although they have the rights and responsibilities...).

4.5c Does the similarity of ideas in sentence 7 and 8 serve as a transitional device from subject A to subject B? What word ties the two sentences together?

4.5d What symbols would you use to describe the paragraph structure?

4.6 Remember that the purpose of a comparison paragraph is to point out the similarities between two subjects. There may be obvious differences between the two subjects, but the similarities are emphasised. With this idea in mind, write two comparison paragraphs on different subjects. The first paragraph should use alternating A and B examples similar to the structure of the model paragraphs 4.1, 4.3, 4.4. The second paragraph should have a series of A examples followed by a series of B examples similar to the structure of the model paragraphs 4.2 or 4.5.

5
Paragraph development by contrast

5.1 Unlike the comparison paragraph, which compares similar aspects of two subjects, the contrast paragraph compares dissimilar aspects of two subjects. Like the comparison paragraph, however, two procedures may be followed in writing the contrast paragraph. The first method alternates examples of subject A with examples of subject B; the contrasts may be in the same sentence, or they may be in consecutive sentences. The other method presents all subject A examples together, then all subject B examples together. The symbols used in previous lessons—TI, TS, A-E..., B-E..., Tr, R—will continue to be used in the structural description of contrast paragraphs.

Where to Study

One major decision which faces the American student ready to begin higher education is the choice of attending a large university or a small college. The large university provides a wide range of specialised departments, as well as numerous courses within such departments. The small college, however, generally provides a limited number of courses and specialisations but offers a better student-faculty ratio, thus permitting individualised attention to students. Because of its large, cosmopolitan student body (often exceeding 20,000) the university exposes its students to many different cultural, social, and extra-curricular programmes. On the other hand, the smaller, more homogeneous student body of the small college affords greater opportunities for direct involvement and individual participation in such activities. Finally, the university closely approximates the real world; it provides a relaxed, impersonal, and sometimes anonymous existence. In contrast, the intimate atmosphere of the small college allows the student four years of structured living in which to contemplate and prepare for the real world. In making his choice among educational institutions the student must, therefore, consider many factors.

5.1a In writing comparison paragraphs, transitional words such as *similarly, also, too, both* are used. For contrast paragraphs, however, other transitional words and phrases are employed: *unlike, on the other hand, in contrast*. Locate the transitional words and phrases used in this paragraph to contrast aspects of the small college and the large university.

5.1b What procedure is used to contrast elements of the two subjects? That is, does the paragraph alternate examples of A and B, or does it list all A examples together, followed by all B examples together?

5.1c What symbols represent the structure of the paragraph? (See exercise 4.4a.)

5.1d Be prepared to discuss in class the meanings of *specialisation, anonymous* (adjective), *anonymity* (noun), *approximate* (adjective), *approximate* (verb), *cosmopolitan, homogeneous,* and *extra-curricular.*

5.2 Read the following partial paragraph. As you read, try to imagine the kind of statement that would be a good topic sentence for the paragraph. Such a sentence should point out the contrasts between the two subjects discussed.

English universities and colleges, because of their selective intake, are relatively small. American universities, which combine a number of different colleges and professional schools, are large, sometimes with 20,000 to 25,000 students on one campus. Teacher training colleges and polytechnics are alternatives to the university course for some students in England, being established for specific purposes. In contrast, virtually all schools of education, engineering and business studies, are integral parts of universities in the United States. In England, universities receive about 70% of their financial support through Parliamentary grants. Similarly, in the United States, public institutions receive about 75% of their funds from local, state, and federal sources, but private colleges and universities receive little or no government support. In England, personal financial aid is provided by the government to over 80% of the students, through local education authorities, according to the parents' income. In the U.S., student aid is administered by the university or the sponsoring agency and is provided by private organisations and the state or federal governments. Obviously, British and American universities have similar educational aims but different means for achieving these aims.

5.2a The topic sentence of this paragraph has been omitted. From the three alternatives given, choose the sentence which most effectively establishes the topic of the paragraph and write it in the space provided above. Be prepared to discuss your reasons for eliminating the two other alternatives.

1 American universities are generally larger than British universities although the quality may be similar.

2 British and American universities are similar in their pursuit of knowledge as a goal but are quite different in their organisation and operation.

3 The organisation, purposes, and operation of universities in England and the United States are very different.

5.2b In the space provided directly above the paragraph, supply an appropriate title.

5.2c What procedure has been followed in presenting the examples in this paragraph?

5.2d Remember that the purpose of a contrast paragraph is to point out differences between two subjects. There may be obvious similarities between the two subjects, but the differences are emphasised. List two similarities between British and American universities. List four differences.

Similarities between British and American universities

_____

_____

Differences between British and American universities

_____

_____

_____

_____

5.3 Read the model paragraph. Notice that all of the information related to subject A is presented first followed by contrasting information related to subject B. Also note that the first and last sentences of the paragraph express essentially the same main idea.

The Objective Test and the Essay Exam

In college and university courses, the objective test and the essay exam are two contrasting methods of evaluation commonly used to measure a student's grasp of subject matter. The objective test usually consists of a large number of unrelated questions that require the student to demonstrate mastery of details. It often leads to rote memorisation of isolated facts during the pre-test period of study. Since the questions on the objective test are presented in true-false or multiple choice form, the student may be encouraged to guess answers for which he has no accurate knowledge. The essay exam, on the other hand, usually consists of a few broadly stated questions that require the student to organise his responses in essay form. Such questions force the student to give proof of his ability to handle general concepts. This type of exam also relies on factual information, but there is far greater necessity for the student to demonstrate analytical and compositional skills. Mere guessing at' answers is reduced to a minimum. Although the objective test and the essay exam have similar goals—the assessment of a student's academic achievement—the techniques (and very often the results) of the two types of examination differ significantly.

5.3a Discuss the following concepts as they are generally used in reference to evaluating student achievement: *objective test, essay exam, rote memorisation, true-false, multiple choice, analytical and compositional skills.*

5.3b Re-read the model paragraph. In the space provided, write short phrases to indicate the main points mentioned to describe the two types of tests.

SUBJECT A THE OBJECTIVE TEST	SUBJECT B THE ESSAY EXAM

5.4 Both the title and the following model paragraph are incomplete. Write the name of your country under the word *and* in the title.

Cultural Differences Between the United States
and

_____

One fascinating benefit of travel to foreign places is learning how customs differ from country to country. As a case in point, there are interesting cultural variations among peoples in such matters as work, play, and education. In the United States, for example, most businesses and industries operate a forty-hour week for their individual employees, although a large number of firms remain open over 100 hours a week by making use of two or three groups of different workers. For leisure-time entertainment, Americans indulge in a great range of sports (hunting, fishing, golf, tennis, baseball, football, etc.) as well as other social and recreational activities participated in by men and women together. The custom of non-separation of the sexes is also the general rule in American schools, from the first grade all the way through the university. _____

_____

_____

_____

_____

_____

_____

_____

_____

_____

Continue the model paragraph in the space provided by writing five sentences:

    1 a transitional sentence that indicates your intention to contrast the American customs discussed in sentences 3–6 above with customs in your country

    2 a sentence on working hours in your country

    3 a sentence on leisure-time activities in your country

    4 a sentence on mixing or separating the sexes in your country

    5 a terminator sentence that makes a general statement about the customs contrasted in the entire paragraph.

5.5   Read the following paragraph. Notice how the two kinds of football games are identified so that the reader is not confused about which game is being discussed.

European Football and American Football

Although European football is the parent of American football, the two games show several major differences. European football, sometimes called association football or soccer, is played in 80 countries, making it the most widely played sport in the world. American football, on the other hand, is popular only in North America (the United States and Canada). Soccer is played by eleven players with a round ball. Football, also played by eleven players in somewhat different positions on the field, is played with an elongated round ball. Soccer has little body contact between players and therefore requires no special protective equipment. Football, in which players make maximum use of body contact to block a running ball-carrier and his team-mates, requires special headgear and padding. In soccer, the ball is advanced toward the goal by kicking it or by butting it with the head. In football, on the other hand, the ball is passed from hand to hand or carried in the hands across the opponent's goal. These are just a few of the features which distinguish association and American football.

5.5a What procedure has been followed in presenting the examples in the paragraph? _____

5.5b In this lesson, three paragraphs (5.1, 5.2, 5.5) use one method of development and two paragraphs (5.3, 5.4) use the other. Which method do you think points up contrasts better?

5.5c What symbols would you use to describe the structure of the paragraph? _____

5.6 Write two contrast paragraphs on topics of your choice. The first paragraph should alternate A and B examples. The second should list together all examples illustrating subject A, then all examples illustrating subject B.

6
Essay development by comparison and contrast

6.1 Carefully study the following model paragraph, which contains important information about the writing process applicable to all kinds of writing, regardless of the method of development.

Editing

Getting your thoughts down on paper is not the final stage of writing a good paragraph or essay. There remains the rewriting of the first draft so as to shape your ideas into a carefully styled composition. Ordinarily, editing involves changes at three points: between sentences, within sentences, and in individual words. At the word level, spelling and capitalisation are checked, but more creatively, words are often changed. A different word may be substituted for the original word because it is easier to understand, is more colourful, gives a more precise meaning, or provides variety. At the sentence level, phrases may be put in a different order, structures of modification revised, different verb structures selected, or the length of phrases or whole sentences may be altered. Finally, for smoothness and balance, changes are made between sentences or paragraphs. Such changes, designed to clarify relationships between ideas, are often accomplished by punctuating more adequately, by introducing more effective transitional devices, or by restating or removing awkward phrases and sentences. Editing then—the self-conscious appraisal and revision of your own work—usually makes the difference between a merely acceptable and a truly superior piece of writing.

6.1a Editing—the rewriting of a first or intermediate draft—may involve changes at three points. Under the following headings, list the ways (suggested in the model paragraph) in which a piece of writing can be improved.

At the word level (sentence 4)

At the sentence level (sentence 6)

_____

_____

_____

_____

Between sentences or paragraphs (sentence 8)

_____

_____

_____

6.1b Does sentence 5 present ways of making editorial changes or does it present reasons for editorial changes?

6.1c Perhaps the easiest way to understand the editing process is to examine several versions of the same paragraph and observe the changes made in each rewrite.

1 The following is an early draft of a paragraph that was satisfactory in its overall organisation. It included topic introducers, a topic sentence, three developers (steps in the process), and a terminator.

Education of a 'Modern' Man

Every age and country has held views on the appropriate education for its young men Education often emphasised much that is traditional, but it is always translated into contemporary terms to help prepare the citizen for life in the 'modern' world. Education typically centred on three aspects of the person's life: his intellect, his body, his morals. Sometimes, the development of ths mind or intellect is stressed to the exclusion of the other aspecte. We may be in such a period now in most countries of the world when education in science and technology is viewed as the primary education of a man. in periods or places of physical strife, the development of the body is seen as the primary necessity for survival. The great periods of exploration and migration emphasised man's physical nature. On the other hand, more tranquil times and places encouraged the education of the citizenry toward the spiritual life. Many of the great religious movements and writings are the result of such education. Although education frequently includes much that is traditional it frequently reinterprets tradition to enable its men and women to meet the modern world on its own terms.

2 Even though the paragraph organisation was adequate, the paragraph could be improved by editing. The edited version is on page 30. Read the paragraph line by line. Which changes represent editing at the word level? The sentence level? Between sentences?

3 The edited version, without editorial marks, appears on page 31.

Education of a 'Modern' Man

Every age and ^(every) country ~~has~~ *have* held views on the appropriate education for ~~its~~ *their* young men *and women* ~~Education often emphasised much that is traditional, but it is always translated into comptemporary terms~~ to help prepare the citizen for life in the 'modern' world. Education typically centre~~d~~*s* on three aspects of the ~~person's life~~ *individuals nature*: his ~~intellect~~ *mind*, his body, his ~~morals. Sometimes,~~ *spirit* *In some periods of history* the development of th~~y~~*e* mind, or intellect, is stressed to the exclusion of the other aspect~~$~~*s*. We may be in such a period ~~now~~ *today* in most countries of the world, when *an intellectual understanding of* ~~education in~~ science and technology is ~~viewed as the primary~~ *the prized mark of an* ~~education of a man.~~ *educated man.* (in periods or places of physical strife *and hardship,* (the development *and well being* of the body is seen as the primary necessity for survival.) The great ~~periods~~ *eras* of exploration, *and* migration, *and military exploitation* emphasise~~d~~ man's physical nature. (On the other hand) more tranquil times and places encourage~~d~~ the education of the citizenry toward the spiritual life. Many of the *world's* great religious ~~movements~~ *monuments* and writings, are the result~~s~~ of such education. Although education ~~frequently~~ *usually* includes much that is traditional, it frequently reinterprets tradition to ~~enable its~~ *instruct* men and women to meet the ~~modern~~ *Contemporary* world on its own terms.

Education of a 'Modern' Man

Every age and every country have held views on the appropriate education for their young men and women to help prepare the citizen for life in the 'modern' world. Education typically centres on three aspects of the individual's nature: his mind, his body, his spirit. In some periods of history, the development of the mind, or intellect, is stressed to the exclusion of the other aspects. We may be in such a period today in most countries of the world, when an intellectual understanding of science and technology is the prized mark of an educated man. The development and well being of the body is seen as the primary necessity for survival in periods or places of physical strife and hardship. The great eras of exploration, migration, and military exploitation emphasise man's physical nature. More tranquil times and places, on the other hand, encourage the education of the citizenry toward the spiritual life. Many of the world's great religious writings and monuments are the results of such education. Although education usually includes much that is traditional, it frequently reinterprets that tradition to instruct men and women to meet the contemporary world on its own terms.

6.2 Often a writer may want to describe several aspects of two subjects that have both similarities and differences. For this purpose, the sentence developers of a paragraph or the paragraph developers of an essay may employ the combined techniques of comparison and contrast. As you read the following essay, carefully examine the various sentences that compare or contrast aspects of the two subjects being discussed.

In the essay, two paragraphs are in a rough draft. Although all the necessary information and ideas are included, paragraphs 2 and 3 can be improved through editing. Paragraphs 1, 4, and 5 have already been edited. Read the essay first for the ideas. You will be asked to do some editing after you finish reading.

Mohandas Gandhi and Martin Luther King

_____ Two twentieth-century leaders who have continued to influence non-violent social protest movements internationally are Mohandas Gandhi and Martin Luther King, Jr. Of different races and cultures, born on opposite sides of the world in nations vastly different in wealth and technology, these two aggressive men in their later years shared the philosophy of non-violent, but direct, action and expended their lives in pursuit of peaceful solutions to social inequities. An examination of their lives, consequently, reveals both similarities and differences in their family backgrounds, ideology, and plans for social action.

_____ Gandhi's and King's family backgrounds show similarities and differences. Gandhi was a Hindi of the Baniyu (Trading) Caste;

his father, nevertheless, was chief minister of the small state of Kathiawad. Gandhi broke with the tradition of his family and went to study law in England at the age of 19, where he had his first contact with western culture. While he read and studied the Bible with interest, he became more deeply convinced of the logicality and profundity of the Hindi religion King was a Black american born into a family of Christian ministers. His father was the pastor of a church which his father-in-law had founded many years before. Unlike Gandhi, King decided to follow in the footsteps of his father and grandfather and study for the ministry. It was only after studying the philosophic words of Plato, Aristotle, Hobbes, Marx, Nietzche, and finally Gandhi, that he began to formulate his own philosophy, which was similar in many respects to Gandhi's. Early environment, family tradition, and study of both Gandhi and King, at some points similar but at most points different, shaped their characters and formed their expectations for their societies and their people.

_____ Both Gandhi and King believed that their aims could be achieved through non-violent means. They held a common ideology of non-violence. This common ideology of non-violence was not to be understood as a failure to act. It should be understood as direct resistance which is grounded in love force or *agraha*. Gandhi said men must resist the evil that men do by refusing to obey a man-made law which contradicted a higher moral law. He often reminded them that blood would have to flow before the Indians attained their ends, but he said the blood must be *their* blood, not the opressors. King cried out, 'I hope no one has to die as a result of our struggle...but if anyone has to die, let it be me'. King reminded Black Americans that they must love their enemies even if it means suffering and death. Similarities in the ideologies of the two men are most apparent since Gandhi was one of the major influences in the development of King's philosophy.

_____ An investigation of the plans for social action of Gandhi and King yields several points of agreement as well as numerous divergences. Gandhi's main concern was to establish India as an independent nation. He wanted to free the people to build and govern India for Indians and not for the use and development of an external power. On the other hand, King's conflict was internal. He sought to achieve justice and equality for Blacks in accordance with the ideals of American democracy. Both men saw the necessity for some kind of economic programme which would make the masses of the poor self-supporting. Gandhi tried to encourage the poor villagers in India to learn to hand-spin cloth as one means of achieving economic independence and cultural solidarity. In a like manner, King urged Blacks to establish transportation and food services which would be supported by the Black community. The economic and social programmes, along with the supportive marches and demonstrations, were important social-action techniques employed by both Gandhi and King as they struggled to improve the quality of life for their oppressed peoples.

_____ Both Gandhi and King were highly respected leaders, whose philosophies were articulated so clearly that they continue to influence contemporary thought and social movements. Their family backgrounds, their belief in the dignity and worth of the individual, and their support of the poor masses led them to lives of non-violent resistance and final martyrdom. But even a superficial examination of their lives reveals differences as well as similarities in their backgrounds and in the development of their influential ideologies.

6.2a Label each paragraph in the model essay using the symbols TP (for topic paragraph), CP (for comparison or contrast paragraph), and RP (for restatement paragraph). Since there are several CP's, number them consecutively CP1, CP2, and so on.

6.2b Underline the sentence that states the main point in CP1. Does the main point of this paragraph come first in the paragraph?

6.2c What form does CP1 have? That is, does it alternate examples A and B, or does it list all A examples together, followed by all B examples together?

6.2d What form does CP2 have?

6.2e Underline the sentence that states the main point in CP3. Does the main point of this paragraph come first?

6.2f What form does CP3 have?

6.2g CP1 has been edited for you. Notice that the changes made follow the suggestions in the model paragraph 6.1 and exercise 6.1a.

1 On page 34 is an early draft of the paragraph that needed only a few editorial changes to make it an acceptable paragraph.

Read through the paragraph carefully and notice the levels at which the changes have been made.

2 The edited version, without editorial marks, appears on page 35.

The ~~Gandhi's and King's~~ family backgrounds show ~~similarities and~~ *of the two men* *obvious parallels* and also striking ~~differences.~~ Gandhi was a Hindu of the Baniyu (Trading) Caste; his father, nevertheless, was chief minister of the small state of Kathiawad; Gandhi broke with the tradition of his family and went to study law in England, at the age of 19, where he had his first contact with western culture. Although ~~While~~ he read and studied the Bible with interest, he became more deeply convinced of the logicality and profundity of the Hindu religion. King was a Black american born into a family of Christian ministers. His father was the pastor of a church which his father-in-law had founded many years before. Unlike Gandhi, King decided to follow in the footsteps of his father and grandfather and study for the ministry. It was only after studying the philosophic works of Plato, Aristotle, Hobbes, Marx, Nietzsche, and finally Gandhi, that he began to formulate his own philosophy, ~~which was similar in many respects to Gandhi's.~~ Early environment, family tradition, and study ~~of both Gandhi and King,~~ at some points similar but at most points different, shaped ~~their~~ the characters *of Gandhi and King* and formed their expectations for their societies and their people.

The family backgrounds of the two men show obvious parallels and also striking differences. Gandhi was a Hindu of the Baniyu (Trading) caste; his father, nevertheless, was chief minister of the small state of Kathiawad. At the age of 19, Gandhi broke with the tradition of his family and went to study law in England, where he had his first contact with Western culture. Although he read and studied the Bible with interest, he became more deeply convinced of the logicality and profundity of the Hindu religion. King was a Black American born into a family of Christian ministers. His father was the pastor of a church which his father-in-law had founded many years before. Unlike Gandhi, King decided to follow in the footsteps of his father and grandfather and study for the ministry. It was only after studying the philosophic words of Plato, Aristotle, Hobbes, Marx, Nietzsche, and finally Gandhi, that he began to formulate his own philosophy. Early environment. family tradition, and study, at some points similar but at most points different, shaped the characters of Gandhi and King and formed their expectations for their societies and their people.

6.2h CP3 is still in a rough draft. Edit the paragraph according to the suggestions in 6.1 and 6.1a.

6.3 The homework for this lesson should be done in three steps.

1 Choose a subject on which you plan to write an essay developed by comparison and contrast. Prepare a short-phrase outline of the ideas or topics you intend to cover. (Review lesson 3, especially 3.3.) Show the outline to your teacher and have it approved before you begin writing your essay.

2 After your outline has been approved, write an essay of from five to ten paragraphs. Closely follow your approved plan of organisation as you expand the phrases of your outline into sentences and paragraphs.

3 After your essay has been read and all points requiring correction marked by your teacher, rewrite the essay making all necessary editorial changes.

As a model for your outline, an outline of essay 6.2 is given below.

Mohandas Gandhi and Martin Luther King
Two twentieth-century leaders
   Different races and culture
   Opposite sides of the world   TP
   Similar philosophies
   Expended their lives in social action

Family Backgrounds
  Gandhi broke with family tradition
  Studied in England
  Retained Hindu religion   CP1
  King kept family tradition, became minister
  Studied philosophy, including Gandhi
  Formed his own philosophy
Ideology of non-violence
  Gandhi said refuse to obey immoral law
  Must not harm oppressors   CP2
  King said he hoped no one would die
  Love one's enemies
Plans for social action
  Gandhi wanted independent India
  King wanted justice in America   CP3
  Gandhi encouraged economic independence and
    cultural solidarity
  King encouraged same for Black Americans
Similarities between Gandhi and King
  As influential leaders
  In family backgrounds   RP
  In times of non-violent resistance
  In service to their people

7
Paragraph development by definition

7.1 Read the model paragraph. As you read, pay close attention to both the meaning and the organisation of the ideas discussed.

The Definition Paragraph

A definition paragraph describes, explains, or defines an unfamiliar term by relating that which is unknown to that which is already known. It makes use of the techniques of comparison, contrast, and synthesis, often in combination. More specifically, a definition paragraph may be developed by using comparison sentences that show that an unknown term is the same as or *like* some known term. Or it may be developed by using contrast sentences that show that an unknown term, though similar in some respects, is basically *unlike* some known term. Or it may be developed by *bringing together* the appropriate like and unlike characteristics of two or more terms to form a new concept, or synthesis. In any case, a given definition paragraph, whether developed by comparison, contrast, or synthesis, or some combination of these, normally ends with a sentence that summarises the distinctive features of the term being defined.

7.1a What three techniques may be used to develop a definition paragraph? (See sentence 2 in the model paragraph.) Restate the idea of sentence 2 in your own words.

7.1b Which sentence explains the technique of synthesis?

7.1c What meaning of the word *synthetic* do you know that often relates to manufactured products?

7.1d What is the function of a terminator in a definition paragraph?

7.2 The definition paragraph is often used at the beginning of a longer paper or book to define a new subject. A psychology textbook might open with a definition paragraph explaining the term *psychology,* a biology textbook with *biology*. Definition paragraphs also serve sometimes as summaries of longer essays or chapters. If the purpose of a chapter in your biology text is to explain or describe the concept of photosynthesis, the final paragraph may be a short definition summarising the major characteristics of photosynthesis.

Photosynthesis

Photosynthesis, which occurs in all land plants and many water plants, is a food-manufacturing process upon which all living things depend. The word is made up of two terms—*photo-,* meaning light, and *-synthesis,* in chemistry meaning the combination of two or more simple elements into a complex chemical compound. More precisely, photosynthesis is the process by which plants use the energy of light to produce compounds, such as sugar and starch, from a number of substances including water and carbon dioxide. In addition to the organic compounds, photosynthesis forms oxygen which is released into the air. In the conversion of light energy into chemical energy, photosynthesis is a primary energy-producing process for all plant and animal life.

7.2a In paragraph 7.1 the unfamiliar term *definition paragraph* is explained or defined in the first sentence. Read it again. Is the unfamiliar term *photosynthesis* defined in the first sentence of paragraph 7.2? What is the function of sentence 1?

7.2b If the term *photosynthesis* is defined in the first sentence, what is the purpose of sentences 2–5?

7.2c What words in the terminator help you refer back to the topic sentence?

7.2d Notice that *photosynthesis* is made up of two parts. Many words in English are formed by combining two root words or a root word plus a prefix or suffix.

In science there are many such words. They are often formed from roots from the Greek and Latin languages. Study the following words in at least two good English dictionaries: *photosynthesis, psychology, biology, dioxide, chemistry, astronaut, cosmonaut, television.* How are the words formed? Can you think of other words in which parts of these words are used? What language or languages do the words come from?

7.3 Definition paragraphs are often used to explain a general concept by using a specific example or occurrence of the concept.

The El Yunque Rain Forest

A rain forest, as the term suggests, is a kind of wooded area, subject to unusually heavy and frequent rains. Found only in the tropical or subtropical regions of the Caribbean, Brazil, Africa, and Asia, rain forests contain a great variety of trees including bamboo, palm, cedar, ebony, calabash, and whitewood. Many of these trees grow to a height of more than a hundred feet, with dense canopies or crowns characteristically forming three distinguishable storeys. Although ground flora is sparse, climbers of all kinds abound, and often exotic flowers appear inconspicuously in the thick foliage. This luxuriant growth results from an annual rainfall in excess of ninety inches, with no dry season. A rain forest of spectacular beauty covers El Yunque, a mountain just outside San Juan, Puerto Rico. The El Yunque rain forest—average rainfall 180 inches per year—is filled with lush, tropical greenery, millions of tiny wild orchids, thirty-foot ferns, and hundreds of varieties of trees and plants, all growing in native splendour.

7.3a The term *rain forest,* defined in this paragraph, is a compound of two familiar words. How are the ideas represented by these two words expanded in the second part of sentence 1?

7.3b Which part of the compound term is developed in sentences 2, 3, and 4? How is this development accomplished?

7.3c Does sentence 5 deal with the same part of the compound term as sentences 2, 3, and 4? How are the two parts of the compound term tied together in sentence 5?

7.3d The first five sentences of the paragraph describe some of the general characteristics of a rain forest. What do sentences 6 and 7 describe?

7.3e In what way does sentence 7 summarise the whole paragraph?

7.3f Previous lessons have made use of special symbols to represent the functions of sentences within a paragraph, or of paragraphs within an essay. These symbols help you visualise the structure or organisation of a paragraph or an essay without longwinded explanations. Symbols make it easier to separate the *function* of an example sentence (E1, E2, E3, E4), for instance, from the *subject matter* (education, background, ideology, career). In themselves, symbols are of little importance; the symbol (TS) or the label (topic sentence) merely gives us a way of discussing the writing process. It is easier to understand the concept *topic sentence* and to discuss its relationship to the function of other sentences in a paragraph, apart from the subject of that sentence. Hopefully, by this time, you are able to think of the organisation or method of development of a paragraph or an essay at the same time as you think about the subject matter you are reading. Although symbols are used sparingly in the remainder of your textbook, you may find it helpful to continue to write the symbols for the model paragraphs or essays as you study them.

7.4 Read the model paragraph. Pay close attention to the kind of developers used.

Nomads

Nomads are people who have no fixed homes but move regularly from place to place. Hunting peoples, such as the Bushmen, Pygmies, and Australian aborigines, move in search of larger animal populations. Pastoral nomads, in the Middle East and Central Asia, move with the seasons to find pasture for their animals. Other pastoral peoples, also dependent on the seasons, cultivate crops but are nomadic when their crops require no attention. Some agricultural workers, in the United States particularly, follow a nomadic life also, migrating northward during the growing and harvesting season and returning to the warmer southern regions in the winter._____

Generally speaking, the nomads' movements are regulated by the seasons and the effects of the seasons on plant and animal life.

7.4a What are the two main characteristics which define *nomad*?

7.4b This paragraph develops the definition of *nomad* through comparison and synthesis. Write an additional developer in the space provided, naming another nomadic group with which you are familiar and explaining why they are nomadic.

7.4c Is your developer adequately summarised by the terminator? That is, are the nomads' movements regulated by the seasons?

7.5 Obsolete words such as *charnel house,* newly created words such as *astronaut* or *cosmonaut,* or foreign words such as *wadi,* frequently require definition by means of another word, a sentence, a paragraph, or a longer explanation. The six sentences below, which are printed in a scrambled sequence, if rearranged would constitute a definition paragraph. In the spaces at the left, write numbers before the sentences to show the sequence in which they would occur in a well-ordered paragraph. The paragraph will then explain a Spanish word which has no exact English equivalent.

Machismo

__The word comes from the Spanish *macho* meaning male, but it suggests greater strength and virility than the English implies.

__The combination of courageous behaviour and earthy sexuality that characterises Latin American manliness is called *machismo*.

__In some situations, it carries the underlying, but usually unstated, notion of masculine charm and even sexual prowess.

__He is boss in his own home, holds his own in manly conversation and activities, defies authority when his individual masculinity is threatened, is stoic in pain, and meets physical danger with aggressive bravery.

__The concept of *machismo* also suggests the proper leadership role that a man plays in his family and in his community.

__ These traits—rugged individual courage and primitive sexual energy in a man, from the village boaster to the national folk hero—are the principal qualities in the concept *machismo*.

7.5a Discuss with your teacher and your classmates your reasons for arranging the sentences in the sequence you determined.

7.5b Read the sentences in the arrangement you have established in order to experience the paragraph as a unified whole.

7.5c What are the two main characteristics of *machismo*? Which sentence in the model paragraph names them?

7.5d Which sentences relate more to the first characteristic? Which to the second?

7.5e What is the transitional word that leads you from the first characteristic to the second characteristic?

7.5f How does the final sentence function as a terminator?

7.5g Discuss the words *virility, prowess, stoic,* and *aggressive bravery*.

7.5h Is there a word or concept similar to *machismo* in your language and culture? Discuss the similarities and differences between your word or concept and *machismo*.

7.6 The techniques of comparison, contrast, and synthesis used in definition paragraphs may be observed in the table on page 42, which shows some of the characteristics of a book, a magazine, and a newspaper. A partial list of defining characteristics is given in the centre column. This list might serve alone as a satisfactory definition through synthesis, but additional information could be provided through comparison and contrast. For instance, a magazine is both similar to and different from a book and a newspaper. *Like* qualities are indicated as + and *unlike* qualities are indicated as − in the chart. Study these characteristics and discuss other qualities which could be added to the list; then write a definition paragraph, using one of the following topic sentences:

1 A book has some of the characteristics of a magazine or newspaper, but it is different from both in several important ways.

2 A magazine has some of the characteristics of a book or newspaper, but it is different from both in several important ways.

3 A newspaper has some of the characteristics of a book or magazine, but it is different from both in several important ways.

KNOWN TERM: BOOK	UNKNOWN TERM: MAGAZINE	KNOWN TERM: NEWSPAPER
+	printed pages	+
−	smooth, thin paper	−
+	cover	−
+	bound	−
+	use of coloured pictures	−
−	advertisements	+
−	multiple authorship	+
−	published regularly	+
−	published weekly	+
−	published monthly	−

8
Paragraph
development by
classification

8.1   Read the following model paragraph.

The Classification of Paragraphs

Individual paragraphs—the building blocks of essays, articles, chapters, and other longer papers—may be classified in a variety of ways. At the essay level, paragraphs may be sorted into functional groups such as introductory, developmental, transitional, summarising, and the like. Depending upon the purpose or intent of the writer, particular paragraphs may be thought of as aiming to persuade, inform, argue, or excite. Paragraphs may also be classified according to such techniques of development as comparison, contrast, and definition. Another developmental device might also be the classification paragraph, which organises items or ideas to be discussed into relatively homogeneous groups. Such classifications make it possible to talk about a large number of paragraphs by grouping them into a small number of classes.

8.1a   Does this paragraph illustrate the developmental technique of classification? What is discussed or classified in the paragraph?

8.1b   Which sentence in the paragraph best defines a classification paragraph?

8.1c   In sentence 3, one way of classifying paragraphs is mentioned. What do you think of the approach mentioned in sentence 3 as a means of teaching and learning concrete writing techniques?

8.1d   Have you found the techniques suggested in sentences 4 and 5 helpful to you in improving your own writing skills? In what ways?

8.2   Although the following paragraph is long, it clearly identifies four classes of words. As you read, observe how the discussion of each class is developed.

Four Classes of Words

As imprecise or gross as classifications sometimes are, they usually indicate classes, or categories, and the labels for these classes that make information more manageable. Frequently, these labels for classes tell us how we are supposed to feel towards a certain thing. The older English dictionaries, for example, classified words and assigned them labels such as *vulgar, dialect, colloquial,* and *slang.* Many commonly used words were labelled *vulgar* and in some dictionaries *low,* implying that only the lowest sort of person used such words. This class of words included most of the 'four-letter words' associated with the bodily functions of sex and elimination. The class of words called *dialect* included expressions commonly used by certain national groups of people or certain regions of the country. People often inferred from the word *dialect* that the English language was improperly learned or used by these speakers; certainly one would not use such a word beyond the borders of that community. *Colloquial* was a less severe label, but it identified words and expressions that might be used in informal educated speech with friends at school, but definitely not in formal compositions. The huge class named *slang* usually meant a word understood by only a select group of people, students for example. Often slang words are quickly forgotten, but they are occasionally taken up by the whole country and soon lose their distinction as slang. The greater social freedom of the past two decades and also the language of public debate have liberated words from such rigid classifications. Modern English dictionaries reflect this variety of usage by employing few classifications that imply social or moral judgment.

8.2a What additional information would you need to write a definition paragraph about the term *colloquial*?

8.2b What is the topic sentence in this paragraph?

8.2c How might the use of a great number of words from these four classes in your writing limit or restrict communication?

8.2d In your native language, are words classified by the same terms discussed in the model paragraph, or are words classified according to a different set of categories?

8.3   The following paragraph is written in a very informal style. Like the other model paragraphs in this lesson, it employs the technique of paragraph development by classification. Notice that the classifications are based on a very limited knowledge possessed by the writer.

Politicians and political parties may be different from country to country, but I know people's political views fall into only three categories. First is the conservative. I haven't travelled much, but in my experience conversatives are all alike no matter where they live. They want to be comfortable, but they don't want to spend much on anyone else's comfort or welfare. Second is the liberal. From what I've read in the newspapers, liberals seem to want the government to do everything. They usually don't have much experience in the real world of hard work. Third is the 'middle-of-the-roader'. Middle-of-the-roaders can't make up their minds about what side to be on. In my opinion, most people are in this class. I don't think I fit any of these categories, but you can place most people into one of these three groups.

8.3a The type of writing you have studied and practised so far in this book is a rather formal style of expository prose. The use of this style of writing is likely to lead to greater success in school. It might be characterised as *academic* prose. Not all expository writing has such a serious purpose or formal style. The methods of development, nonetheless, in both formal and informal writing are often the same. What makes paragraph 8.3 informal?

8.3b Which sentence tells you that this is going to be a classification paragraph? How does it tell you?

8.3c In the space provided directly above the paragraph, supply an appropriate title.

8.3d In a classification paragraph, it is important to set up adequate categories and equally important to define what goes into these categories. Classification of people that is based on superficial evidence and that is too rigid or too general is called stereotyping. What words or phrases in the model paragraph indicate that the classification is based on limited or incorrect observation?

8.4 Notice the use of transitional devices in the following model of a classification paragraph.

Each year the car industry throughout the world produces a glittering array of different models, designed to appeal to every age, to every taste, to every pocketbook. For the person who needs reliable transportation at minimum operating cost, there is a large selection of small, lightweight cars that travel great distances on very little petrol. For the young, who demand the ultimate in appearance and performance, there is a great variety of sports and speciality models. For the 'young at heart'—the middle-aged, middle-class citizen who wants a prestige mix of style, size, and comfort—there is a wide range of big, sleek cars available with all sorts of optional equipment. And finally, for the truly wealthy, there is a select group of luxury cars, custom-built to the most fastidious taste. On the basis of just these four categories, it can be said that the car industry exemplifies the seller's slogan, 'You pay your money, and you take your choice.'

8.4a   In the blank space on the right in the Table, list the categories of cars described in the model paragraph in relation to the classes of people on the left.

CLASSES OF PEOPLE	TYPES OF VEHICLES
the economy minded the young the middle-aged, middle-class the rich	

8.4b   Extend the two classification lists above by adding other groups of people and cars.

8.4c   Write an appropriate title in the blank space provided.

8.5   The following paragraph is taken from the second edition of a popular textbook published in several languages besides English. It classifies the various activities of the psychologist into three major enterprises.

> Psychology, as defined, comprises a number of different kinds of enterprises, so different that they may seem to have nothing in common. One psychologist is engaged in vocational guidance; he spends his day talking to high school students, studying their academic records and their test scores and from these, in principle, showing the student how to clarify his own ideas about his future training and occupation. Another spends his day studying delayed reaction in goldfish or the navigation of bats. Other psychologists are assisting in the diagnosis of neurotic patients, doing research on the childhood experiences that contribute to neurosis, or taking part in combined research on the effects of tranquillisers. But all such disparate activities have this in common, that the methods derive from the same fundamental training in the procedures and conceptions of academic psychology, and that the worker is either putting the conceptions to practical use or trying to improve on them (or both).[1]

8.5a   Which sentence explains what various psychologists' activities have in common?

8.5b   The three classes of psychologists' work are not clearly named in the paragraph. Discuss the activities of each class to determine what distinguishes one from another.

8.5c   Indicate the phrase that relates the topic introducer and the terminator in this paragraph.

[1] Hebb, D.O. *A Textbook of Psychology,* Second Edition, W.B. Saunders Company, Philadelphia, 1966, page 310.

8.5d Using a good dictionary, decide what less formal words or expressions might be substituted for the following words in the model paragraph: *comprises, enterprises, neurosis, disparate, conceptions.*

8.6 Remember that the purpose of a classification paragraph is to group a large number of items or ideas into a small number of classes. With this in mind, write two classification paragraphs on different subjects. The first paragraph should use an informal style of first person observations, such as, 'I believe there are only three types of teachers in the world'. (Review 8.3.) The second paragraph should use a more formal academic style. (Review 8.1, 8.2.)

9
Essay development by definition and classification

9.1 After reading the following paragraph, write a short phrase outline noting the key ideas expressed in each of the five sentences.

Subjects in British Universities

The typical academic programme for university students in Great Britain is composed of a varying number of courses or subjects within a field of specialisation. The academic obligations for each subject fall into three broad types. Lectures, at which attendance is not always compulsory, often outline the general scope of the subject matter and stress the particular specialisation of the lecturer. Tutorials, through individual or group discussion, reading extensively, and writing essays under the tutor's direction, ensure focused and in-depth understanding of the subject. Examinations on each subject require the student to consolidate his knowledge of the subject, which he has gained through lectures, discussions and a great deal of independent study. These three categories of academic activity—lectures, tutorials and examinations—provide the means by which students prepare themselves in specialised fields of knowledge in British universities.

9.2 Edit the following paragraph. Remember that editing usually involves improvements in punctuation, capitalisation, spelling, word choice, transitional devices, modification, word or phrase position or deletion.

Although vastly different, both human beings and animals	1
organise into groups and follow certain fixed behaviour in	2
carrying out their roles in life. In most human societies for	3
example behaviour related to sex roles is specific to each culture	4
with the appropriate behaviuor related to courtship, marriage,	5
and sexual relations specified by the society. In the animal	6
world, behaviour varies from species to species but each have	7
its own pattern of courtship and mating, some approaching	8
the complexity and stability of human groups. Human beings	9
vary in their care of their children, but all human beings take	10
care of their children for long periods of time, some until	11
adolesence or marriage, others until education is finished or	12
jobs are secured. animal groups too have different ways of	13

caring for their young with some pushing their young out of 14
the nest early and others keeping their young beside them in 15
the herd for many years. Persons select leaders or leaders 16
emerge from the group and then dominate it through physical 17
intellectual, or spiritual force. Animals too follow the strongest 18
or oldest leader of the pack or the herd. Perhaps the most 19
complex behaviour in human groups is in the division of work 20
to insure that both the intelectual and physical tasks of the 21
society are carried out. Some animal groups divide the work 22
of the community (not always equally, notably bees and some 23
birds) among various members of the group. It should be 24
clear that human beings and animals show simularities in the 25
social organisation of their groups from these limited examples. 26

Make the necessary editorial changes to improve the paragraph. The
line in which the change is to be made is given for your help.

> Commas—lines 3, 4, 14, 17 and 26
> Capitalisation—line 13
> Spelling—lines 5, 12, 21 and 25
> Repetitious transitional device—line 18
> Bad position of phrase—line 26
> Un-needed word or phrase—lines 10 and 11
> Word repetition—lines 14 and 15
> Weak modification—line 23 and 24
> Poor choice of words—line 16
> Subject-verb agreement—line 7

9.3 Often a writer employs more than one method of development
in an essay. He may, for instance, decide to *classify* objects, events,
or terms in order to make it easier for the reader to retain a few classes
rather than many specific items. Additionally, he may need to *define*
the labels he uses in classifying the subject, especially if these labels
are not widely known or are abstract.

The following essay combines the techniques of definition and
classification to discuss one of the problems sometimes encountered
in research papers or other academic and professional writing. After
you have read the essay once, re-read each paragraph carefully to
determine the method of development used.

Plagiarism in the Academic Community

Scholars, writers, and teachers in the modern academic community have strong feelings about acknowledging the use of
another person's ideas. In the English-speaking world, the term
plagiarism is used to label the practice of not giving credit for
the source of one's ideas. Simply stated, plagiarism is 'the wrong-
ful appropriation or purloining, and publication as one's own,
of the ideas, or the expression of ideas (literary, artistic, musical,

mechanical, etc.) of another'.[1] From an ancient Latin word meaning to kidnap or steal the child or slave of another, plagiarism is universally condemned in the modern academic world. It is equivalent to stealing the livelihood or savings of a worker, for it robs the original writer or scholar of the ideas and words by which he makes a living.

The penalties for plagiarism vary from situation to situation. In many universities, the punishment may range from failure in a particular course to expulsion from the university. In the literary world, where writers are protected from plagiarism by international copyright laws,[2] the penalty may range from a small fine to imprisonment and a ruined career. Protection of scholars and writers, through the copyright laws and through the social pressures of the academic and literary communities, is a relatively recent concept. Such social pressures and copyright laws require writers to give scrupulous attention to documentation of their sources.

Students, as inexperienced scholars themselves, must avoid various types of plagiarism by being self-critical in their use of other scholars' ideas and by giving appropriate credit for the source of borrowed ideas and words. There are at least three classifications of plagiarism as it is revealed in students' inexactness in identifying sources properly. These categories, which will be discussed in some detail in succeeding paragraphs, are plagiarism by accident, by ignorance, and by intention.

Plagiarism by accident, or oversight, sometimes is the result of the writer's inability to decide or remember where the idea came from. He may have read it long ago, heard it in a lecture since forgotten, or acquired it second-hand or third-hand from discussions with colleagues. He may also have difficulty in deciding whether the idea is such common knowledge that no reference to the original source is needed. Although this type of plagiarism is the least serious, it must be guarded against. If the idea, or the words used to label or express it, is unique, the writer must make an effort to identify the source.

Plagiarism through ignorance is simply a way of saying that inexperienced writers often do not know how or when to acknowledge their sources. The techniques for documentation—note-taking, quoting, footnoting, listing bibliography—are easily learned and can prevent the writer from making unknowing mistakes or omissions in his references. Although 'there is no copyright in news, or in ideas, only in the expression of them',[3] the writer cannot plead ignorance when his sources for ideas are challenged.

---

[1] *Oxford English Dictionary,* London, 1933.
[2] See 'copyright,' *Encyclopedia Britannica,* Chicago, 1968.
[3] 'Copyright,' *The New Caxton Encyclopedia,* London, 1969.

The most serious kind of academic thievery is plagiarism by intention. The writer, limited by his laziness and dullness, copies the thoughts and language of others and claims them for his own. He not only steals, he tries to deceive the reader into believing the ideas are original. Such words as *immoral, dishonest, offensive,* and *despicable* are used to describe the practice of plagiarism by intention.

The opposite of plagiarism is acknowledgement. All mature and trustworthy writers make use of the ideas of others but they are careful to acknowledge their indebtedness to their sources. Students, as developing scholars, writers, teachers, and professional leaders, should recognise and assume their responsibility to document all sources from which language and thoughts are borrowed. Other members of the profession will not only respect the scholarship, they will admire the humility and honesty.

9.3a What is the function of paragraph 1?

9.3b Which paragraph largely defines the term *plagiarism*?

9.3c What are the three classifications of plagiarism mentioned in the essay?

9.3d What is the TS of paragraph 2?

9.3e What method of development is used in paragraph 3?

9.3f What method of development is used in paragraphs 4, 5, 6?

9.3g Which paragraph defines *copyright laws*? Do you feel it is a complete explanation? Why?

9.3h What is the opposite of *plagiarism*? Which paragraph defines this concept?

9.3i Is the final paragraph an effective terminator for the essay? Why?

9.3j Read paragraphs 1 and 7 again (first and last). Can these two paragraphs stand alone as an essay? What ideas are included in paragraphs 2 through 6 that make the essay more informative?

9.4 Write an essay of six or seven paragraphs in which you use the techniques of definition and classification. You may want to expand one of the topics discussed in 7 or 8 or any of the topics suggested in other lessons of the book that lend themselves to development through definition and classification.

10
Paragraph development by space and time

10.1 The following paragraphs demonstrate the development of topics according to space arrangements and time sequences. In some instances, the subject may require the organisation of ideas based on space or spatial relationships, without reference to time. In discussing a contemporary topic such as the world population problem, you might write about events in South America, India, Japan, Europe, and Africa with no specific reference to the dates of the events. Another subject may demand an organisation based on the chronology of events with little or no reference to where the events took place. The biography of a national political figure might stress a man's election to the governing body in 1933, his appointment as a minister in 1942, a personal scandal in 1956, re-election in 1960, and so on, irrespective of the place in which these events occurred, either because the place is obvious or because it is not significant. Other subjects, major historical events for example, may require a method of development using both space and time relationships.

The first model paragraph demonstrates development through spatial relationships in a very small area. Try to visualise a painting of a mountain landscape as you read.

Looking at a Painting

A painting, among other things, is a controlled or confined space, and our appreciation of a painting partially depends on how well we perceive the spatial relationships employed by the painter. To begin with, our vision is restricted or directed by the outer limits of the painting, a frame in most instances. We may perceive the painting as a 'whole,' but most often our eyes are directed by the painter to a focal point or centre of interest. The focus of the picture alone would not hold our attention, however. We are led to it by the painter because of its significance through its relation to other objects in the painting. We might, for example, notice an outstanding face in the background in the midst of dark clothing and shadows. Or we see figures in the distance in the painting's perspective, in contrast to a flat silhouette in the foreground that frames them. We are compelled to look at the clouds in the sky because our eyes are lifted upward by the lines of the trees or mountains in the painting. We observe that a large brown field in the lower left is balanced with a small, colourful cluster of trees on the right. In the end—especially in traditional or representational painting—we always return to the centre of interest, which has been intensified for us by our taking in the details which visually support it.

10.1a Before you attempt the following exercises, spend some time in looking at paintings and discussing with your classmates and teacher the artist's organisation of spatial relationships.

10.1b What is the relationship between the main idea of sentence 2 (framing) and the main idea in the first part of sentence 1 (controlled space)?

10.1c Some of the artist's techniques are only indirectly suggested in the paragraph. Which sentence indicates his use of colour? Of perspective? Of light?

10.1d According to the paragraph, what effect does observation of the details of spatial organisation in relation to the central focus have on the viewer?

10.1e All of the following words have rather special meanings in a discussion of painting. Check your dictionary to clarify the meanings of *spatial, perceive, focal point, focus, perspective, silhouette, representational, background, foreground*.

10.2 A common example of paragraph development by time is a short biography which is best organised according to important dates. The events of the person's life are listed sequentially within a clearly observable time frame.

William Shakespeare

William Shakespeare, the greatest literary genius of the English language, was born in Stratford-on-Avon in 1564. Although Shakespeare is principally remembered today as the premier English dramatist, he early attained widespread popularity in the 1590's as a lyric and narrative poet with the publication of *Venus and Adonis* (1593) and *The Rape of Lucrece* (1594). He first attained success as a playwright after the production of *Henry IV, Part I,* in 1592. Over the next two decades he wrote a succession of widely acclaimed plays which may be categorised roughly into three groups: histories, comedies, and tragedies or tragi-comedies. Among the history plays, *Richard III* in 1592–93, *Richard II* in 1594–95, and *Henry V* in 1599 were especially well received and have continued to be produced even until the present day. Of the comedies, *A Midsummer Night's Dream* (1595), *The Merchant of Venice* (1595–96), and *Much Ado About Nothing* (1598), were and are enduring favourites with actors and audiences alike. But undoubtedly Shakespeare's world-wide reputation as a dramatist rests on the profound exploration of the human condition portrayed in his great tragedies *Romeo and Juliet* (1594–95), *Othello* (1602), *Hamlet* (1602), *King Lear* (1606) and *Anthony and Cleopatra* (1607). After having dominated the London theatrical scene for some twenty years, Shakespeare retired to Stratford, where he lived in relative ease and comfort until his death in 1616.

10.2a Which two dates indicate the limits of the time frame in this short biography? In what way are these dates analogous to the frame of a painting?

10.2b While the dates of the biography are generally listed from early to later time, four sub-groups of dates are mentioned. What kinds of literary works are described within these four sub-groups? How does the grouping of dates according to literary types aid the reader?

10.2c Are the dates mentioned in relation to the several literary genres listed in chronological order? How does such listing aid the reader?

10.3 Although dates are indicated in the following paragraph, they are not stressed. Notice as you read that the method of development, based on geographical space, stresses the movement and wide range of Alexander's conquests rather than what happened on what date in each place.

Alexander the Great

Whether he was moved simply by curiosity or by a thirst for conquest, one of the most fascinating and controversial figures in world history was Alexander the Great. From his first battle, the capture of Athens in 338 B.C., until his death thirty-two years later from a fever in Babylon, Alexander had personally led his armies across most of his known world. Like an enormous harvesting machine, Alexander and his armies moved from his home in Macedon south into Greece, across the sea to the lands east of the Mediterranean, and down into Egypt. Consuming the wealth and experiences of the East while, at the same time, spreading the language and culture of Greece, he crossed the ancient Persian Empire through central Asia and on into India, his conquests including large portions of the three continents of Europe, Africa, and Asia. His empire was so vast that on his death it was divided into five parts, each under the administration of one of his generals. Alexander is regarded in legend and history as both hero and ruthless conqueror, with mothers in central Asia still naming their sons after him but also using his name, when children misbehave, to instill fear in their hearts.

10.3a Which sentence first indicates that the paragraph is developed by space? What words or phrases accomplish this?

10.3b What words or phrases in sentence 4 relate to the concept of *harvesting machine* in sentence 3?

10.3c Is the final sentence an adequate terminator? Why?

10.3d Referring to the map below, discuss the conquests of Alexander in relation to the sequence of geographical areas mentioned in the model paragraph. The numbers on the map refer to locations mentioned in the paragraph. How does the organisation of the material presented in the model paragraph reflect a logical spatial relationship?

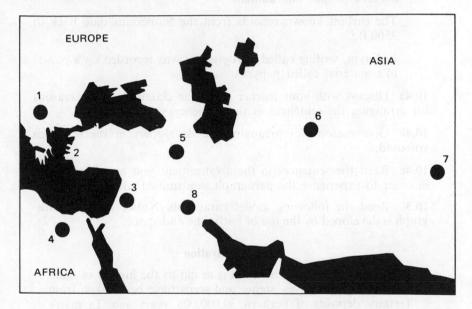

10.4 The ten sentences below, which are printed in a scrambled sequence, if rearranged would constitute a paragraph developed by time. In the spaces at the left, number the sentences in the sequence in which they would occur in a well ordered paragraph.

The Birth of Writing

___In what is now Iraq, the ancient Sumerian people developed a writing system called *cuneiform,* which used a small wedge-shaped instrument to make marks or impressions in soft clay.

___Chinese writing began as early as 2000 B.C.

___The first real alphabet, in which one written symbol stood for one sound of the language, was developed by the Phoenicians.

___Several ancient civilisations developed writing systems.

___All alphabetic writing has its origin in this Phoenician improvement in writing of about 1100 B.C.

___No matter what language one speaks today, the writing system probably began with one of these ancient systems for recording the events of its speakers' lives.

___Egyptians used papyrus as far back as 2500 B.C.

___In the Far East, the Chinese invented a system of writing which used pictograms, that is simplified representations of familiar objects, people, and animals.

___The earliest known records from the Sumerians date back to 3500 B.C.

___In Egypt, writing called *hieroglyphics* was recorded on a paper-like material called papyrus.

10.4a Discuss with your teacher and your classmates your reasons for arranging the sentences in the sequence you determined.

10.4b Give reasons for arranging the developers in the sequence you used.

10.4c Read the sentences in the arrangement you have established in order to experience the paragraph as a unified whole.

10.5 Read the following model paragraph. Notice that the paragraph is developed by the use of both time and space.

Grape Cultivation

The history of grape cultivation is as old as the history of man. Fossilised grape leaves, stems, and seeds have been taken from Tertiary deposits of perhaps 30,000,000 years ago. In man's recorded history, we have details of grape and wine production depicted in Egyptian mosaics of 2400 B.C. It is theorised that cultivation of the grape originated in the area around the Caspian Sea and from there grape growing spread to Asia Minor and Greece. In Homer's time, about 1000 B.C., wine was a common feature of Greek life. From Greece, grape culture spread to Sicily. The Phoenicians took the grape to France as early as 600 B.C.. Pliny, writing before A.D. 100, described ninety-one varieties of grapes and fifty kinds of wine. The Romans planted grapes along the River Rhine in Germany by A.D. 200 and probably took them to England as well. Columbus, and later the colonists of the seventeenth and eighteenth centuries, brought the European grape to America, where it was crossed with the disease-resistant, native, wild American varieties. In modern times, the grape is cultivated in the temperate zones on every continent, and grapes or their products are consumed throughout the world.

10.5a Which sentence first indicates that the paragraph includes information based on space?

10.5b Look up the meanings of the following words: *fossilised, Tertiary, mosaics, theorised.*

10.5c In a simple tabular form, list in the blanks below all places with corresponding dates mentioned either directly or indirectly in the paragraph. Notice there are more places than dates mentioned. Even though both time and space are useful methods of development in this paragraph, they do not receive equal emphasis.

GRAPE CULTIVATION	
PLACE	YEAR

10.5d Read the following paragraph and compare it with your chart in 10.5c.

One theory is that cultivation of the grape originated in the area around the Caspian Sea. From there grape growing spread to neighbouring areas of Asia Minor, then to Greece, and from Greece to Sicily. The Phoenicians took the grape into France, and the Romans planted grapes in Germany and England. At the same time as grape cultivation spread into the West, grapes were carried into the East by way of India. Everywhere that new lands were settled, people took the grape along. Columbus and later colonists brought the European grape to America, where it had little success until it was crossed with tne native American varieties.

1 What is the method of development, time or space?

2 What kind of information in your table in 10.5c is largely omitted in the developmental technique in paragraph 10.5d?

10.5e Read the following paragraph and compare it with your table in 10.5c.

The history of the grape is as old as man, and older. In fact, fossilised grape leaves, stems, and seeds have been taken from Tertiary deposits of perhaps 30,000,000 years ago. But in man's recorded history, we have details of grape and wine production depicted in mosaics of 2400 B.C. during the Fourth Dynasty of Egypt. In Homer's time, about 1000 B.C., wine was a common feature of Greek life. By 600 B.C., grapes were known in France, and no later than A.D. 200 they were introduced into Germany. The writer Pliny, before A.D. 100, described ninety-one varieties of grapes and fifty kinds of wine. Columbus, and later the colonists, brought European grapes to America, where they found native varieties already growing in a wild state.

1 What is the method of development?
2 What kind of information in your table in 10.5c is largely omitted in the developmental technique in the paragraph in 10.5e?

10.5f Which of the three paragraphs about the cultivation of grapes (10.5, 10.5d, 10.5e) do you feel is most successful? Why?

10.6 A paragraph developed by space is an attempt to create in words a visual sense of an area. It cannot duplicate what one could actually see if one were on the spot, but, nevertheless, it has certain advantages. It can indicate a point of view, direct the reader's attention, and restrict his vision in a certain direction or in a special sequence. In a paragraph describing your university, you might develop the paragraph by space in several different ways:

1 You might use some important landmark, for example the Administration Building, and describe other locations in relation to it. The order in which you discuss each location is not as important as its relationship to the landmark.

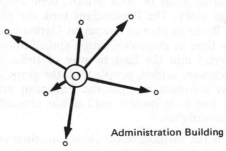

Administration Building

2 You might use an important landmark as the starting point and move from it to the next location, on to another, and so on, perhaps ending back at the original landmark.

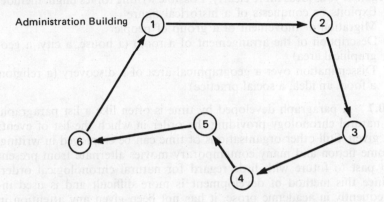

3 Another type of development by space might stress the boundaries of an area. The order in which these are listed is not necessarily important so long as there is a logical progression from location to location.

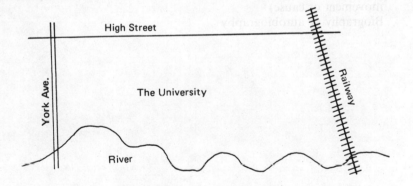

4 Still another spatial development might stress the inter-relationships between locations. The order is not necessarily important.

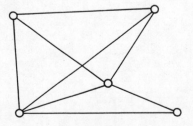

Write a paragraph developed by space. Use one of the methods just described to develop your paragraph. Try to visualise the spatial organisation before you write. A diagram or drawing might help you organise your ideas more clearly. Possible writing topics might include:

Exploits or conquests of a historical figure

Migration or movement of a group of people

Description of the arrangement of a room (a house, a city, a geographical area)

Dissemination over a geographical area of a discovery (a religion, a food, an idea, a social practice)

10.7   A paragraph developed by time is often like a list paragraph, a natural chronology providing the order in which the list of events is given. Still other organisations of time can be employed in writing. Some fiction and many contemporary movies alternate from present to past to future with little regard for natural chronological order. Since this method of development is more difficult and is used infrequently in academic prose, it has not been given any attention in your book.

Write a paragraph developed by time. Use a natural chronological order for the events you select. Possible writing topics might include:

Important events of the day (week, month, year, decade)

Development of an industry (an institution, a state, a sport, a movement or cause)

Biography or autobiography

11
Paragraph development by process description

11.1 Process description is similar to the procedures followed in conducting a scientific experiment. It describes definite steps in a necessary order. Keep this comparison in mind as you read the model paragraph.

Water Purification

The provision of safe water necessitates one of the major expenditures of manpower and revenue in our modern cities. The purification of water is basically a two-step or three-step process carried out under the strict supervision of public health scientists and engineers. As the first step, natural water from the least contaminated source is allowed to stand in large reservoirs, where most of the mud, clay, and silt settle out; this is called 'sedimentation'. Often in water with high mud content, lime and aluminium sulphate are added to the water in the settling reservoirs. These chemicals react in the water to form aluminium hydroxide, which settles slowly and carries much of the suspended material, including most of the bacteria, to the bottom of the reservoirs. As the second step, the water is filtered through beds of sand and gravel, which remove other impurities and chemicals in it. During or after filtration, chemicals are ordinarily added to the water to kill any remaining harmful bacteria. Chlorine is one of the most common chemicals used for this purpose. A third step taken by some municipalities is adding to the water other beneficial chemicals such as fluoride to make tooth enamel hard, and soda ash to make the water itself soft. The water purification process, carried out with little variation from one large city to another, is perhaps the biggest factor in the prevention of major outbreaks of disease in this country.

11.1a What is the function of sentence 1? If you had read only sentence 1 and stopped, without knowing the content of the rest of the paragraph, what are several different ways of continuing the paragraph? If this were a simple list paragraph, you might proceed as follows:

The provision of safe water results in one of the major expenditures...

Another major expenditure is allocated to the maintenance of good roads...

11.1b What is the function of sentence 2? How does this sentence rule out most of the possibilities for continuing the paragraph discussed in 11.1a? What key words in the sentence determine the content and development procedure of the paragraph?

11.1c Sentences 3, 6, and 9 introduce the different steps in the water-purification process. What function do the intervening sentences serve that distinguishes the process paragraph from the simple list paragraph?

11.1d What words or phrases in the terminator relate it to the topic sentence?

11.1e In the model paragraphs of lessons 1 and 2, the points or examples used as developers have no necessary order or sequence. With very slight changes of transitional devices, points or examples might be presented in a very different order with no essential change of meaning in the paragraph as a whole. Can the same be said of the process paragraph? Why?

11.2 The organisation of the following paragraph is somewhat different from most of the models in this book. It does, however, have all of the requirements of a good paragraph including a topic sentence.

Industrialisation

The first stage in the process of industrialisation for most countries is the discovery of new sources of raw materials and fuel. The second is the reorganisation of the labour force from one that is rural and agricultural to one that is urban and industrial. Concurrent or subsequent to the development of industries and factories, the third step is the creation or expansion of communication and transportation systems. Many socio-economic-cultural changes follow quickly behind the technological changes, and must be considered a part of the industrialisation process. One of the first social changes is the shift of population from rural areas to the cities where the factories are located. Technology is then applied to agriculture, resulting in greater production of food for the urban populations but requiring fewer agricultural workers. These changes often result in a redistribution of wealth, especially the decline of land as the sole source of wealth, and new economic and political power based on industry. Finally, there are changes that effect the world community as it tries to contain or control the aspirations and needs of individuals and nations. Industrialisation is a complex technological and cultural process that shows remarkable similarities no matter where or when it takes place.

11.2a In most of the paragraphs you have studied, the topic sentence has appeared at or near the beginning of the paragraph. Which sentence in this paragraph is the topic sentence?

11.2b The three steps in the process of water purification described in 11.1 are clearly marked by obvious enumerative phrases. How many distinct steps are described in the process of industrialisation? What are the enumerative or transitional phrases that move the reader from one step in the process to another?

11.2c What is the function of sentence 4?

11.2d Since the topic sentence comes at the end of the paragraph, what additional function does it serve besides being the topic sentence?

11.3 Read the following excerpt adapted from a popular chemistry textbook. It describes the process of scientific investigation.

The Scientific Method

The heart of any study of the physical universe lies in observation and generalisation. The observed phenomena are organised into coherent patterns or generalised statements. The intellectual steps or processes involved in this study have traditionally been placed in an 'ideal' order and called the scientific method.

(1) *Observations,* often in the form of experiments, are made on the physical system being studied.

(2) An attempt is made to find a pattern of consistency in all observations of the physical system under study. If it is possible to formulate a verbal or mathematical statement which relates the observations, that statement is called a *law.*

(3) An imagined picture or model of the system is constructed mentally with the stipulation that the behaviour of the imagined model conforms to the observed law. Such a model and its suggested behaviour constitute a *hypothesis.*

(4) A good hypothesis often suggests other behaviour of the system which may be tested by further observation. A hypothesis whose predictions conform to observations, or which has been moulded and modified by testing, evolves into a *theory* of the behaviour of the system in question.[1]

_____

[1] 'The Scientific Method' was adapted from Harry B. Gray and Gilbert P. Haight, Jr. *Basic Principles of Chemistry,* W.A. Benjamin, Inc., New York, 1967, page 2.

11.3a Often a process paragraph in a technical or scientific textbook uses numbers to indicate the steps of a process. Some writers feel that the numbering technique makes the process clearer. Others prefer to use phrasal transitions from step to step. Re-read the model paragraph inserting in place of the numbers at the beginning of each step the following transitional words.

As the first step,
Using the data of the first step,
Next,
And finally,

11.3b Which procedure—numbers or transitional words—makes the material easier to understand for you? Why?

11.3c Since the paragraph does not have a terminator, in the space provided write one that satisfactorily concludes the discussion. The terminator in a process paragraph is frequently a summary statement. In this case, *observation, law, hypothesis, theory* might appear in the terminator.

11.3d The forms of the following nouns are plural and require plural verbs. Look up the singular forms in your dictionary.

phenomena
data
processes
hypotheses

11.4 Read the following paragraph. Which sentence tells you the method of development will be process-description?

Cheesemaking

Hundreds of different names for cheese are used throughout the world, but the general principles of making cheese from milk have changed little for nearly 3000 years. The aroma, texture, and taste of cheese depend on slight variations of the process used to produce it, but all methods consist of two to four basic steps. The first step consists of the coagulation of the protein 'casein' by adding acid or enzyme to the milk, usually cow's milk, but sometimes the milk of the sheep, goat, mare, ass, reindeer, llama, yak, camel, or buffalo. Next the liquid, called whey, is drained, leaving a semi-solid cheese, called curds, which may be eaten in this form or processed further. All soft or cream cheeses are of this type. Hard cheese undergoes two additional steps in the process. The semi-solid cheese is matured until it reaches the required level of acidity, at which time it is salted and pressed into forms or moulds to give it the distinctive shape and size of a particular cheese. The final step is the aging process during which the world's most famous cheeses acquire their unique flavours from the place and length of storage. Changes in the manufacture and storage produce different kinds of cheese, but cheese is one of the universal foods from the regions of the world where milk-producing mammals live and varies only slightly in the basic manufacturing process.

11.4a What is the function of sentence 2?

11.4b What is the function of sentence 5? How does it refer back to sentences 2 to 4?

11.4c What is the function of sentence 6? How does it refer back to sentences 2 to 4?

11.4d Slight variations of the process used in cheesemaking may change the taste of the cheese. What might happen if the steps described in the paragraph were completely changed or done in a different order?

11.4e What words or phrases in the terminator relate it to the TI and TS?

11.5 In a well constructed process description, the topic sentence establishes the context of the process developed in succeeding sentences. Notice that the process of preparing for examinations is divided into two major stages although there are several steps in the process.

Preparing for Final Examinations

The process of preparing for end of year examinations involves both long-range and short-range planning. Basic long-range considerations are regular class attendance and consistent, week-by-week completion of all reading assignments. Of course, systematic notes or outlines of major points raised in the class discussions or in the assigned readings provide a condensed record of the essential facts and concepts. To keep outlines and notes up to date, they should be reviewed and revised from time to time throughout the college year. Short-range planning should include collecting copies of previous examinations or suggested study questions at least three weeks prior to the examination date. These can be used as guides in an intensive review of the ideas that teachers have considered important. Self-confidence in analytical and compositional skill can be increased by actually writing out and checking practice answers to typical examination questions. Finally, in addition to preparing the mind, care should be taken to ensure that the body is well-rested and nerves calm at the actual time of examination. From the foregoing, it should be clear that effective preparation for final examinations is really a year-long process requiring the continuous use of appropriate study techniques.

11.5a Why does the author divide the process into long-range and short-range planning?

11.5b What is the function of sentence 2? How does it refer back to the TS?

11.5c What is the function of sentence 3? How does it refer back to sentence 2?

11.5d What is the function of sentence 4? How does it refer back to the TS?

11.5e Is the final sentence an adequate terminator?

11.6 Write a process-description paragraph employing the techniques illustrated in this lesson. Write a first draft of your paragraph. After a period of time, perhaps a day, write an edited final version of your paragraph. Turn in both versions of this writing exercise. The following topics may help you get started.

Preparing a speech (a lesson, a demonstration)

Teaching someone to swim (ride a bicycle, play an indoor or outdoor game, drive, cook)

The modernisation of areas (schools, laws)

12
Essay
development by
time, space and
process

12.1 In lesson 9 you studied an essay that employed two major methods of development. The following essay combines the techniques of time, space, and process, as well as definition, to discuss a historical event. The complexity of the various elements and influences making up the subject matter requires a combination of developmental techniques. After you have read the essay once, re-read each paragraph carefully to determine the method of development used.

Pre-Columbian Settlement of the Americas

Europeans are usually given credit for the discovery of the New World, that is, the Western Hemisphere. We now believe, however, that it was 'discovered' a number of times by European, Mediterranean, and African adventurers. We use the term *New World*—newly discovered and unsettled—in contrast with *Old World*—meaning the then known world of written historical records and literatures. In the period immediately after Columbus' accidental discovery, the major influences on the American continents were European, and for the people in Europe, America was a new world. For the people who lived in America at the time, however, it was the only world in their memory.

Before Columbus, the most noted 'discoverer' of America, arrived in the New World, several flourishing civilisations had existed for centuries. The earliest inhabitants of America may have arrived over 25,000 years before Columbus. It is certain that men lived in what is now Nevada by 9,000 B.C. Beginning in 8,000 B.C., when the climate began to warm up, hunters ranged over portions of the entire New World in search of animals and other food. Between 3,000 and 2,000 B.C., men had begun to settle in communities where they carried on some farming and fishing. Remains from the first large building projects, from 500 B.C. to 500 A.D., consist of large ceremonial earthworks or mounds. By the time Columbus reached the New World in 1492, the American civilisations had reached a level of culture which included personal wealth, fine buildings, expert craftsmanship, and religions which structured the daily lives of the people.

___ Continuing archeological excavations tell us what little we know about the extent of these earliest immigrants. The most advanced cultures developed in what is now Mexico and Peru. Many of the surrounding peoples in Central America, South America, and North America also reached complex states of civilisation, but were largely isolated from each other and from the greater civilisations of the continents. Widely separated peoples reached similar stages of development independently but during the same periods of time. For instance, the mound builders made burial and ceremonial sites in several places in the eastern U.S., central Mexico, and on the Gulf of Mexico, all at about the same time. Men settled down to plant crops, especially maize, in Peru, Central America, and the eastern U.S., again during the same period. But from the earliest archeological evidence of men in America, we know that they ranged over the entire hemisphere, from Alaska to Tierra del Fuego.

___ The most popular theory regarding the origins of the first settlers of the New World is that they crossed over from Asia to Alaska, which was connected by land at that time. Pushed out of Asia by some unknown natural or social forces, these hardy emigrants peopled the New World and started it on a path of cultural development independent of anything in Asia or Europe of the same periods. The search for a more hospitable climate and necessary food forced many of the new arrivals to continue their walk to the opposite end of the hemisphere. Along the way, groups of people stopped or split off to continue in separate directions, leaving isolated groups, or tribes, throughout North and South America.

___ The dispersal of the original people is one of the most interesting areas for speculation. Although there are few facts, we can reconstruct what might have happened. There were, no doubt, small numbers of people. When groups separated from one another, they quickly became isolated, lost in the vast wildernesses of empty continents. The small bands looked for food and for a less hostile environment, moving frequently during the early centuries. Enough of them adapted to their cruel surroundings to populate even the most severe climate and terrain of the new lands, but many moved on. Internal strife within tribes probably forced others to seek new domains. The first several millennia, then, were characterised by the continual shifting of peoples in search of a better life.

___ By the time the Spanish, led by Hernando Cortes, destroyed the Aztec empire in 1521, some cultures of America equalled the landmarks of European civilisations. These Pre-Columbian civilisations, independent of the technological and social developments of other continents and quite unlike the European cultures who conquered them, were a 'new world' for their discoverers. It should be remembered, however, that this new world was already peopled throughout by groups whose personal achievements and cultural history were vigorous, rich, and peculiar to the Americas.[1]

12.1a Label each paragraph in the model essay using the terms studied so far to describe methods of development and structural function. For example, process, time, space, classification, definition, comparison, contrast, and so on; or topic paragraph, restatement paragraph, and so on.

12.1b Which paragraph defines *New World*? After reading the essay, do you feel this is a good term? Why?

12.1c The term *Pre-Columbian* is not defined in the essay. Can you explain its meaning?

12.1d Review 10.6. Which type of spatial relationship is used in paragraph 3 of 12.1?

12.1e The method of development in paragraphs 4 and 5 is the same—process. On what environmental conditions is the process based?

12.2 Write an essay of five to ten paragraphs in which you use the techniques of space, time, process, and any other method of development thus far discussed in this book. The essay should convey an overall sense of movement through time or space or a progression through the steps of a process description. Individual paragraphs may support this overall development by definition, classification, comparison, and so on. Avoid mixing too many methods of development, however, for the essay may then lack focus. You may want to use a topic of your own choice, or one of the topics suggested in 10.7 and 11.6, or any of the topics mentioned in other lessons of the book that lend themselves to development through space, time, and process. Before you write your essay you may find it helpful to make an outline of the ideas you intend to cover.

[1] Information from Bushnell, G.H.S. *The First Americans: The Pre-Columbian Civilizations,* Thames and Hudson, 1968.

13
Paragraph development by cause and effect

13.1 The stating of facts and the giving of reasons to explain why or how the facts came about is the basic procedure in paragraph development by cause and effect. Observe the procedure as you read the following paragraph.

Slaughter on the Highways

During the past five years, the number of Americans killed annually in car accidents has climbed to more than 55,000. This needless slaughter on streets and highways can be attributed to three general causes. Mechanical failures, especially those related to faulty brakes and bald tyres, account for a significant number of fatal accidents. Environmental conditions such as blind corners, narrow streets, heavy fog, intermittent rain or snow resulting in slippery roads also contribute to the grisly accident statistics. But without doubt the most frequently reported factors in car accidents are errors of human judgment— all the way from such follies as excessive speed and drunken driving to such momentary lapses as failure to signal a turn or a change from one lane to another. The man behind the wheel is often his own worst enemy.

13.1a In which sentences do you find the causes in this paragraph?

13.1b In which sentence do you find the effect?

13.1c What is the function of sentence 2?

13.1d The last sentence in the paragraph neither states a cause nor an effect. What is its function?

13.2 The next model paragraph demonstrates a rather straightforward development, listing three causes of language change.

Language Change

There are many reasons why languages change, but three major causes help illustrate the concept. Initially, various languages that started from the same parent developed their own uniqueness after groups of speakers drifted away from one another to establish isolated, independent communities. Another major cause of language change is the influence of and interaction with foreign cultures, often as a result of military conquest. A continuing cause for change is rapidly expanding technology and new systems of communication that bring all cultures and languages into closer contact, with borrowing between languages a common phenomenon in the contemporary world. All languages change as the experiences of their speakers change.

13.2a What is the function of sentence 1? Do you feel it is effective? Why?

13.2b The three causes of language change mentioned in the model paragraph are not introduced by such repetitious introductory phrases as 'one cause...another cause is....' Can you list each cause in a few words?

_____

_____

_____

_____

13.2c In the last sentence, how does 'the experiences of their speakers' summarise the causes?

13.2d How does the terminator refer back to sentence 1?

13.3 The following fragment has the basic structure of a cause and effect paragraph. Read it and plan an appropriate completion of the causal relationships suggested in the last sentence.

Causes of Student Failure

Thirty-six per cent of the freshmen entering a large New York university are dismissed during or at the end of the first year. Studies indicate that this alarming rate of failure is due to a variety of causes, some of which are beyond the control of the student. Among these are inadequate academic and personal counselling services, inferior quality of instruction in very large freshman classes, and the computerised anonymity of most administrative procedures. But many of the causes of early student failure can be traced to non-adaptive behaviour on the part of the student himself._____

_____

_____

_____

_____

_____

13.3a In the space provided, write three sentences that give reasons for student failure in the first year of college. Remember that these reasons must be factors within the students' control.

13.3b Write an appropriate terminator for this paragraph.

13.3c Which sentences in the paragraph state the causes? Which state the effect?

13.3d What is the function of sentences 2 and 4?

13.4 The technique of cause and effect has great flexibility, for the relationships between causes and effects are not always as clear-cut as the two terms seem to suggest. Causes may not all carry the same weight, for example. Several contributing causes may be grouped together to form one important cause. There may be one effect to a cause, or there may be many. Effects may be less important than causes. And so on. The next few model paragraphs, selected from textbooks, further demonstrate cause and effect in the kind of academic writing you are likely to read. They show considerable variety in their methods of indicating the relationships between causes and effects. Because the paragraphs are taken out of context, the method of paragraph development may seem less obvious; as you learned in the model essays, one paragraph in a longer paper builds on the previous paragraphs and anticipates the next. Exercises are therefore kept to a minimum, discussing only the most obvious features of the paragraph.

> Several factors cause fatigue, but in general, they come down to two main causes: lack of fuel or food, and the excessive accumulation of by-products of activity. Muscle activity uses up stores of glycogen or sugar. It also must have oxygen, for a muscle deprived of it will soon cease to contract. Lactic acid and carbon dioxide are the chief by-products of muscle activity, but there are also toxins from other sources which may help produce fatigue. Some of these toxins may come from bodily infections and some may be absorbed from breathing or from the digestive process. But in addition to these factors, there are certain causes of fatigue which are more or less obscure. Some of these are less physiological than psychological, such as lack of interest in what you are doing. When you do something that bores you, you tire easily; if you are interested in your work, you forget the amount of energy you put into it. You also tire more quickly when standing than when you are walking, for in walking, each leg rests half of the time.[1]

13.4a The topic sentence indicates there are two main causes of fatigue. Which sentence indicates that still other causes are going to be discussed?

13.4b Does the paragraph have an effective terminator?

[1] Hickman, C.P. *Health for College Students,* Second Edition, Prentice-Hall, 1963, page 126.

13.4c Although this paragraph is clearly organised, it also seems to suffer from fatigue. Can you explain why the paragraph seems 'tired'?

13.5 The method of development in the following paragraph demonstrates another variation of the cause-and-effect relationship. Read the paragraph carefully.

> There has been an emphasis, recently, on the possibility that society itself, or the group culture, may be producing the distortions of personality, mental illness, and emotional instability which apparently are widespread. Various writers have pointed out that man's basic needs are being extensively thwarted by the demands of society. According to this view, man no longer may be an individual or develop his imagination, reason, and creative powers; and he is prevented, because of society's compartmentalising, from achieving feelings of relatedness—of loving and being loved. Because of the competitive demands of civilisation, man now strives for 'things' rather than for his own development. He feels himself to be merely a pawn rather than a contributing member of society. If he rebels, he is subject to punishment by society, or if, on the other hand, he submits, he may become simply a stereotyped, pedestrian member of society and thus lose much of his urge toward creativity and individuality. As an example, Fromm suggests that society produces in its members what he calls 'a socially patterned defect'.[1]

13.5a In which sentence is the cause-and-effect relationship first indicated? Is it the topic sentence?

13.5b Explain how the phrase 'socially patterned defect' summarises the whole paragraph and refers back to the topic sentence.

13.6 The subject of the following paragraph, the growth of the labour force in the nineteenth century, is not specifically mentioned until near the end of the paragraph. Does it seem to be a cause or an effect?

> With the beginning of the factory system, labour needs could be met in part by long working hours. In an economy where agriculture prevailed, it was not unusual that factory operators should insist upon sunrise to sunset as a normal working day. Factory labour was at first recruited from the women and children in the towns and villages surrounding the factory areas. The first persons employed in the Slater (textile) mills, for example, were seven boys and two girls between the ages of seven and twelve. In the Massachusetts mills, the general policy

[1] Thorpe, L.P. *The Psychology of Mental Health,* Second Edition, The Ronald Press Company, New York, 1960, page 18.

was to employ female operatives who were boarded at company houses and subjected to considerable company control in so far as conduct was concerned. Such employments, significant as they might have been, were a 'drop in the bucket' in terms of labour requirements. The explanation of labour force growth in the nineteenth century is closely related to the history of the population growth that occurred. An important element in the population growth was the tide of immigrants who came to the United States in increasing numbers until government policy discouraged large-scale immigration after the first world war.[1]

13.6a List the three causes for the growth of the labour force discussed in the model paragraph.

_____

_____

_____

13.6b Do the three causes seem to receive equal emphasis?

13.6c What is the function of sentence 6?

13.7   Cause and effect is an extremely advantageous developmental technique in longer papers. The model paragraph in 4.5 discussed the migration of Southern blacks and Puerto Ricans to New York City. This subject could be given greater scope by indicating several of the causes for the migration. Paragraph 11.2 discussed the process of industrialisation resulting in greater urbanisation. This subject could be enlarged upon by a discussion of the many causes for urbanisation in modern societies.

As you have seen in the model paragraphs in lesson 13, cause and effect can be used in developing individual paragraphs on a variety of subjects. This technique is appropriate for subject matter ranging from the rather trivial 'Why I Like Sports' to more serious topics such as 'The Causes of Influenza as a World Health Problem'.

Write two cause-and-effect paragraphs on any two of the following topics or others of your own choice:

Major causes of crime (or poverty, or pollution) in my city

Success in college

The rise and fall of skirt lengths

[1] Cohen, S. *Labor in the United States,* Second Edition, Charles E. Merrill Books, Inc., 1966, page 11.

14
Paragraph development by generalisation

14.1 Paragraph development by generalisation is very much like paragraph development by examples (see lesson 2). Both make use of developers, which are examples supporting an idea or point of view. One common difference is that the generalisation is stated as a *conclusion* based on several examples, given as facts or opinions, which *lead* the reader to make the same conclusion. The focus of the reader's attention is on the generalisation. It is less like telling the reader 'This is true because of this and this and this' and more like saying 'If this is true, and this and this, then we can make the following *general conclusion,* can't we?'

Following is a slightly adapted version of the model paragraph in 2.1. Compare this version, which illustrates development by generalisation, with the original in lesson 2.

Effective Writing—A Must in Universities

In preparing scientific reports of laboratory experiments, a student must present his findings in logical order and clear language if he wants to receive a favourable evaluation of his work. Similarly, in order to write successful answers to essay questions on history or anthropology examinations, a student must arrange the relevant facts and opinions according to some accepted pattern of paragraph structure. And certainly when a student writes a book report for English, or a critique for political studies, or a term paper for sociology, style and organisation are often as important as content. Clearly, the ability to write well organised, concise paragraphs and essays is essential to a student's success in almost all university courses.

Examine the next paragraph which also uses examples to lead to a generalisation.

Impact of Science on Agriculture

Science and technology have contributed in several important ways to the improvement of agricultural production. Scientifically compounded fertilisers make the land more productive. Chemical insecticides and pesticides, applied periodically to growing crops, selectively destroy a wide range of detrimental insects and pests. The numerous herbicides now available eliminate unwanted grasses and weeds, freeing field crops for more abundant growth. Research in plant sciences has created hybrids which provide higher-yielding plant strains and seeds. Moreover, technology has developed various kinds of machines such as tractors and combines, which perform many time-consuming tasks that once required a great deal of manual labour. Hydroelectric installations supply water for advanced irrigation techniques and power for the complex needs of the modern farm. Plainly, large scale agricultural production in the 1970's depends heavily on developments in science and technology.

14.2 The following paragraph describes the effects of large industries in an urban setting on small owner-operated shops.

The Decline of Small Businesses

Each year, countless small businesses close their doors and go into bankruptcy. The corner grocer, the little dress shop, the locally owned sandwich shop, the baker, the dancing school, the beauty salon, all are victims of the constantly shifting economy. They are, at times, replaced by other small businesses that temporarily fill the needs of the neighbourhood but frequently end up sharing the same fate of dissolution. More often, the market served by the small business is taken over by a large store or plant, frequently from a more distant place of operation. Typically, the corner grocer's and baker's business has already gone to the nationally owned supermarket down the street. The woman who runs the dress shop chooses fashions out of tune with the times and gets too old to keep the store open during the most convenient hours for shoppers, who then go off to the big department stores. It is increasingly difficult, apparently, for small businesses to succeed in our complex economic structure based, as it is, on small profit margins and tremendous sales volume.

14.2a What is the function of sentence 1?

14.2b Sentence 1 is a statement of observable fact that could be supported with statistics from cities and countries throughout the world. Compare sentence 1 with the final sentence. How do they differ? What factors are stated in the generalisation that do not appear in sentence 1?

14.2c What kind of information do the developers provide that leads to the generalisations?

14.2d Point out words or phrases in sentences 2 to 6 that lead you to accept the generalisation, especially the final phrase of the generalisation: '... complex economic structure based, as it is, on small profit margins and tremendous sales volume'.

14.3 The following incomplete paragraph leads you to make your own generalisation. On the basis of the causal examples given in the paragraph and other observations of your own, what would you conclude about *news*?

The News Broadcast

Turn on the world news broadcast any evening, and the predominant mood is one of gloom. Maybe Brazil and Peru haven't gone to war, but the news is that some other countries have. Thousands of people have been left homeless by earthquakes, floods, and fires, but nobody reports on the millions of people unharmed by natural disasters. In the cities, men and women go about the daily affairs of earning a living, quietly and calmly, without making the news, but crime, greed, and corruption seem to be on every street corner according to the latest news report.

———————————————————————

———————————————————————
———————————————————————
———————————————————————

14.3a Notice that each developer includes one item of what might be considered good news and one item of bad news. In the space provided, add one more sentence that contrasts bad news and good news.

14.3b Which news—good or bad—dominates in the paragraph and, apparently, in news broadcasts generally?

14.3c Complete the paragraph with an appropriate generalisation. Since the major generalisation in this paragraph, as in 14.1, comes at the end, remember that it should also be an effective terminator.

14.3d What words or phrases in your final sentence refer back to sentence 1?

14.4 Paragraph development by generalisation is employed for a variety of reasons. It may be used to gently persuade and lead the reader to the writer's point of view. It may establish rapport by stating a conclusion that is rather obvious and already agreeable to both reader and writer. It may point out a foregone conclusion or generalisation upon which the writer wishes to build additional information and opinions. For these purposes, and others as well, authors of the type of material you will be reading in your academic course work often use generalisations. The following model paragraphs are excerpts from popular textbooks in such subjects as geography, English language, and sociology. They exemplify a wide variety of generalisations, and as in lesson 13, exercises are kept to a minimum.

The surface of the earth is chiefly water—something that we, as dwellers on the land, are apt to ignore or completely forget. As noted earlier, the Pacific Ocean alone covers nearly one third of the globe. The combined areas of all water bodies, including oceans, seas, and lakes, add up to nearly two and one-half times that of all the land of the earth. In other words, about 71 per cent of the earth's surface is water. In addition to the large expanses just mentioned, there are small ponds, waters that run as streams on top of the land, and other waters that lie or move within the upper portion of the earth's crust. And there is water in vapour and condensed forms in the atmosphere. Thus, water is an important and practically all-pervasive element in man's habitat.[1]

14.4a Which sentence states the generalisation in this model paragraph?

14.4b The structure of this paragraph is very similar to the model paragraph in 14.1. Sentence 1 begins with a statement of observable fact. Compare sentence 1 with the final sentence. How do the two sentences differ? How is the relationship between the two indicated?

14.5 The following paragraph contains three related generalisations. As you read the paragraph, try to discover the way in which these generalisations are interrelated.

When most of us think about language, we think first about words. Thus, the hardest part of learning a foreign language may seem to be memorising its vocabulary; when we observe a child first acquiring speech, we talk of his progress as a matter of learning new words. We are also likely to feel that the adult speaker with the largest vocabulary has the best command of English. To think of a language as just a stock of words is, however, quite wrong. Words alone do not make a language; a grammar is needed to combine them in some intelligible way. Moreover, words are relatively easy to learn, and indeed all of us go on learning them all our lives. They are also the least stable part of language. Words come into being, change their pronunciations and meanings, and disappear completely—all with comparative ease. Yet it is true that the vocabulary is the focus of language. It is in words that sounds and meanings interlock to allow us to communicate with one another, and it is words that we arrange together to make sentences, conversations, and discourse of all kinds. Thus we have a paradox in that the most ephemeral part of language is also the centre

[1] Kendall, H.W., Glendinning, R.H. and MacFadden, C.H. *Introduction to Physical Geography*, Harcourt Brace Jovanovich, Inc., 1970, page 96.

where meaning, pronunciation, and grammar come together.[1]

14.5a Which sentence states the first generalisation?

14.5b Which sentence provides a transition from the first generalisation toward the second?

14.5c Which sentence states the second generalisation?

14.5d In what way does the third generalisation make use of the first two?

14.5e This paragraph exemplifies a very persuasive technique using generalisations. Notice that the first generalisation, which, as the authors indicate, everyone believes, is stated initially so that the authors can knock it down later with a second generalisation. The second states a different point of view although it is still incomplete. The authors are able, in the final sentence, to make the defensible third statement that clearly represents the authors' views. As you can observe in the paragraph, it is an interesting and effective technique for leading the reader to a modified point of view or a new understanding of the subject.

14.6 The following model paragraph is taken out of context from a sociology textbook. The generalisation is about education as a means of social control. Notice that there are two aspects of the generalisation stated in the first sentence.

Education in a broad sense, from infancy to adulthood, is thus a vital means of social control, and its significance has been greatly enhanced in the last two decades by the rapid expansion of education at all levels in the developing countries, and by the equally rapid growth of secondary and higher education in the industrial countries. Through education new generations learn the social norms and the penalties for infringing them; they are instructed also in their 'station and its duties' within the system of social differentiation and stratification. In modern societies, where formal education becomes predominant, and where an important occupational group of teachers comes into existence, education is also a major type of social control (as the source of scientific knowledge) which is in competition and sometimes in conflict with other types of control. This conflict may become particularly acute with the extension of higher education to a much larger proportion of the population, as the experience of the last few years has shown in Europe and North America; and the educational system may increasingly

[1] Pyles, T. and Algeo, J. *English: An Introduction to Language*, Harcourt Brace Jovanovich, Inc., 1970, page 96.

provide one of the main sources of change and innovation in the social norms.[1]

14.6a What are the two aspects of the generalisation in sentence 1?

14.6b In sentence 3, point out words or phrases which refer to *social control*.

14.7 Generalisations, as we have pointed out in this lesson, are based on several examples or instances that lead the writer and reader to form a conclusion. You could write a generalisation based on only one example, but the conclusion would be less convincing unless it were already self-evident or were some universal truth. The sentence containing the generalisation may appear at the beginning or the end of a paragraph, but in the planning stage you normally think of the generalisation first. Then you develop the examples that can effectively lead up to the generalisation. Remember that the main purpose of the generalisation paragraph is to convince the reader that your conclusion is the only logical one.

Write two generalisation paragraphs on two different topics selected from the following or on other topics of your choice.

> Social (or economic, or educational) problems in my country
>   (in developing countries, in industrial countries)
> Life in the 1980's (the twentieth century, the city)
> On being twenty years old (young, old)
> Woman's role (in the future, in marriage)

[1] Bottomore, T.B. *Sociology: A Guide to Problems and Literature,* Second Edition, George Allen & Unwin Ltd., 1971.

15
Essay development by various means

The exercises included in this lesson are intended to summarise the methods of paragraph and essay development illustrated throughout this book and to illustrate the manner by which several methods may be combined in one essay. The organisational techniques of comparison, contrast, definition, time and space, process, etc., that you have studied and practised in individual lessons, do indeed appear regularly in the formal prose of educated writers. This lesson provides an opportunity to observe various developmental procedures as they are employed *naturally* by mature writers.

15.1   The following short essay was written with two purposes in view: (1) to supply some interesting information about the growth and spread of the English language, and (2) to review some of the paragraph development techniques presented in earlier lessons. At the end of each paragraph, write the term that best describes the predominant method of development used.

Speech Communities

There is no denying that English is a useful language. The people who speak English today make up the largest speech community in the world with the exception of speakers of Mandarin Chinese. Originally they were small tribes of people living in northern Europe who left their homelands and settled in England. Isolated in their island community, the various tribes used languages which became more and more similar to each other and less and less like the other languages of Europe. Eventually, the language had enough uniformity to be used by all speakers in England. The people were united into a speech community through their shared language. In time, people moved from the small island to many parts of the world, taking their language with them and thus still remaining members of the English speech community wherever they settled._____

A speech community is similar to other kinds of communities. The people who make up the community share a common language. Often they live side by side as they do in a neighbourhood, a village, or a city. More often they form a whole country. Many nations are composed of a single major speech community, for example, Italy, Sweden, and Japan. National boundaries, however, are not always the same as the boundaries of a speech community. Some nations (for example, Russia and India) are made up of many speech communities. Some speech communities (for example, Arabic, Spanish, and English) extend across national boundaries. A speech community, then, is any group of people who speak the same language no matter where they happen to live._____

We may say that anyone who speaks English belongs to the English speech community. For convenience, we may classify the speakers into two groups: one in which the speakers use English as their native language, the other in which the speakers learn English as a second language for the purposes of education, commerce, and so on. In the former group we, obviously, would include England, Canada, the United States, Australia and New Zealand. Naturally, not all people in these countries speak English natively, but a large majority do. In the latter groups we would include, among many others, India, Denmark, Kenya, Burma, Turkey, Ethiopia, and the Philippines. Not all these countries use English for the same purpose or to the same extent, but each uses English for important social and commercial activities._____

English serves as a functional alternative language in several areas of public activity for the many nations of the world which use it as an international second language. Because of its widespread use geographically, and because of the large number of people who speak it, it has been adopted as the language of aviation and air traffic. English has continued as one of the important languages of commerce, as the sphere of political and economic influence of the English-speaking nations has extended beyond the boundaries of England. The use of English in international diplomacy is strengthened by its acceptance as one of the official languages of the United Nations. And as a final example, English is the language of the majority of published materials in the world so that education, especially specialised higher education, has come to rely on an understanding of English very heavily. In no sense does English replace the cultural heritage and emotional ties of the first language, but for many speakers throughout the world, it provides a means of communicating with people of similar training and interests who would otherwise not comprehend them._____

Learning a second language extends one's vision and expands the mind. Looking at the world or oneself through a different language system shows the limits of one's own perception and adds new dimensions to familiar objects or events. A second language teaches us different ways of labelling and organising our experiences. The history and literature of a second language record the real and fictional lives of a people and their culture;

a knowledge of them adds to our ability to understand and to feel as they feel. Learning English as a second language provides another means of communication through which the window of the entire English speech community becomes a part of your heritage. _____

15.2 Select a short article from an English language news or commentary magazine.

1 Does the article follow one predominant method of development? That is, does it mainly compare, or give examples or define, etc?

2 Can you identify individual paragraphs which follow the methods studied in this book?

3 Do some methods seem to carry on over more than one paragraph? Give an example.

4 Is the terminator a restatement? How does it conclude the article?

15.3 Choose one of your textbooks written in English or a book in your field of interest from the library. Select a chapter you have already read or would like to read. Choose every fourth paragraph for analysis.

1 Identify the method of development used in each paragraph, if possible.

2 Describe how each paragraph is related to the paragraph immediately preceeding it and following it.

3 Do some paragraphs use more than one method of development?

4 Are there some paragraphs that do not seem to follow the methods of development studied? Can you explain how they are developed?

5 Copy the paragraph that you think is organised best. Bring it to the class for discussion.

15.4 Read a feature story in an English language newspaper, a Sunday newspaper or magazine, or a popular magazine about general subjects. Choose something which interests you.

1 What method of development does the author use in the first paragraph?

2 How does the author catch your interest in the first paragraph?

3 Does the first paragraph tell you what the remainder of the article is going to be about?

4 Does it show you what method of development will be followed in the remainder of the article?

5 In what way does the subject matter of the article determine which method of development is used? For example, a biography of

a famous person would include some paragraphs using time as a method of development.

15.5 Read an article from a technical journal (for example, science, engineering, medicine, education, etc.).

1 Does the article follow one predominant method of development?

2 How does the method (or methods) seem to relate to the subject matter?

3 Copy the paragraph that you think is organised best. Bring it to the class for discussion.

4 Are there some paragraphs that do not seem to follow the methods of development studied? If there are, bring one example to the class for discussion.

5 Do some paragraphs use more than one method of development? If so, bring one example to the class for discussion.

15.6 Write a short essay about the place you would most like to visit. Your essay might include paragraphs on the following topics among others:

Identify the place by type or category.	CLASSIFICATION
Tell how you became interested in it.	PROCESS
Give a brief history.	TIME
Mention something about its physical characteristics or boundaries.	SPACE
State reasons for your interest.	CAUSE or LIST
State reasons for its present or historical importance.	CAUSE, EFFECT or EXAMPLE
Tell how it compares with other places you know about.	COMPARISON or CONTRAST

15.7 Write a short essay about one aspect of your chosen field of study. Your essay might include paragraphs of the following types:

DEFINITION of the field or your area of interest within the field.

LIST the various branches or divisions which make up the field.

EXAMPLES of the contributions of the field.

COMPARE or CONTRAST your field with another or others.

Explain an important PROCESS or method in your field.

List CAUSES for interest in the field.

List EFFECTS of studying in your field.

Answers to the Exercises

Specific answers are given for most questions in the text. Example answers are given for questions for which there may be a variety of answers depending on the readers' experiences. No answers are given where the answer is totally dependent upon information only the reader can supply.

1.1a

sentences in paragraphs four functions	1
introducers establish topic focus	2
developers present details	3
modulators provide transition	4
terminators conclude ideas	5
paragraphs four sentence types	6

1.1b They present details. Numbers 2, 3, 4, and 5 in the outline above.
1.1c They provide transition. No. No.
1.1d Yes. It refers to the first sentence—the introducer—by mentioning four sentence types and by mentioning successful, that is well written paragraphs.
1.1e Transitional words *first, second, third,* and *fourth.* It is noted later that this technique provides rather uninteresting transitions.

1.2a Yes. Introducer—sentence 1; developers—sentences 2, 3, 5; and terminator—sentence 6.
1.2b Sentence 4.
1.2c Yes. It refers to the 1960's, European colonialists, and the birth of African nations.

1.3a No. Only one developer is not sufficient to support the paragraph introducer.
1.3b Example: Secondly, Indonesia has a GNP of $11,100,000,000 and a population of 122,864,000 inhabitants scattered over approximately 3,000 islands including Java, Sumatra, Kalimantan, Sulawesi, and West Irian. Thirdly, Japan has a GNP of $124,700,000,000 and a population of 104,649,000 living on approximately 1,000 islands the largest of which are Honshu, Kyushu, Hokkaido, and Shikoku.

1.4a Introducer. It establishes the topic focus or idea of the whole paragraph.

1.4b Developers. They present details that support or give additional information.

1.4c Sentence 6. It connects terms for cooking methods and terms for behaviour.

1.4d *For example* begins a list of cooking terms
another lists a second example
A related process lists another example and refers back to the previous ones
Still another lists a fourth example.

1.4e Terminator. It rounds off the paragraph by referring back to cooking terms and special meanings.

1.5a Example: In addition, creativity will be required to meet the constantly changing world around us. Finally, perseverance, the ability to hold on at all costs, will be required in a society where competition for space, food, and shelter will increase with a growing population.

1.5b Examples: Essential Qualities for the 1980's
Personal Qualities for Success in the 1980's
Personal Success in the 1980's

2.1a

ability to write essential	1
reports logical order clear language	2
answers accepted pattern of structure	3
style and organisation important	4
skill in writing crucial	5

2.1c Sentence 1.

2.1d Sentence 2 is a specific example of the general idea expressed in sentence 1.

2.1e Sentence 3 is a specific example of the general idea expressed in sentence 1. Sentences 2 and 3 are both specific examples.

2.1f Yes. Key words in the terminator are *successful achievement...
university subjects* which refer to the introducer *student's success
...university courses.*

2.2a 6, 5, 4, 2, 3, 1.

2.2b TS / E1, E2, E3, E4 / R.

2.2c All the example sentences list types of manual labour.

2.2d The development or progress of a country depends on manual labour.

2.2e *To begin with* indicates the first example. *Secondly* comes next. Since *finally* introduces the last example, the third example must be the sentence beginning *And of course...*

2.2f   Example: National Development and Manual Labour
        Manual Labour and Industrial Development

2.3a   Example: Modern literature in most countries deals with real
        social issues.
2.3b   Example: It is clear from these limited examples that contem-
        porary literature in many parts of the world deals with the social
        issues of the day.
2.3c   TS / E1, E2, E3, E4 / R.

2.4a   Example: Most societies have some means of law enforcement.
2.4b   Example: Although vastly different in form and in circum-
        stances, most cultures have ways of enforcing laws agreed upon
        by the society.
2.4c   Example: Law Enforcement
        Universal Law Enforcement
2.4d   TS / E1, E2, E3, E4 / R.

2.5a   TS / E1, E2, E3, E4 / R.
2.5b   US advanced educational opportunities _____ 1

            general education liberal arts colleges _____ 2

            technical education specialised schools _____ 3

            two-year community colleges _____ 4

            technical institutes by businesses and industries ___ 5

        educational opportunities continue for years _____ 6

3.1a   1. TS; 2. E1; 3. E2; 4. E3; 5. E4; 6. R.
3.1b   Topic sentence. It introduces the subject of qualities important
        in the successful job interview.
3.1c   They provide specific examples of the important qualities.
3.1d   Yes. It provides a satisfying conclusion to the paragraph by
        referring back to the topic introduced in sentence 1.
3.1f   successful interview requires certain qualities _____ 1

            well-groomed and modestly dressed _____ 2

            manner of speaking _____ 3

            talk knowledgeably about position _____ 4

            self-confidence and enthusiasm _____ 5

        these characteristics make successful interview _____ 6

3.2a   TP, EP1, EP2, EP3, EP4, RP.

3.2b   Underline sentence 1 in the TP. Yes.

3.2c   Underline sentence 1 in EP1. Yes.

3.2d   They state specific examples to support the main idea expressed in the topic sentence of EP1.

3.2e   Underline sentence 1 in EP2. Underline sentence 2 in EP3. Underline sentence 1 in EP4. In EP3, the topic sentence follows a topic introducer.

3.2f   They state specific examples to support the topic sentences.

3.2g   Underline the final sentence in the final paragraph. No, it comes last. It summarises the other sentences in the paragraph. Yes, it refers back to the topic paragraph by mentioning *success in interview*.

3.2h   It makes the essay more personal for the reader. It generalises the ideas, that is, it makes the qualities refer to all successful job applicants. The final sentence again reminds the reader that the qualities mentioned in the essay refer to himself and all other job applicants.

4.1a   Yes. Sentence 1 serves as topic sentence. Sentences 2–7 are developers, the final sentence is a terminator.

4.1b   Sentence 2 is A (paragraph)–E1. Sentence 3 is B (essay)–E1. Sentence 4 is A–E2; sentence 5 is B–E2. Sentence 6 is A–E3; sentence 7 is B–E3. There is logical alternation.

4.1c   A–E1—For example, the paragraph. . .
B–E1—In the essay. . .
A–E2—Next. . .
B–E2—Similarly. . .
A–E3—Finally. . . the paragraph.
B–E3—The essay, too. . .

4.1d   Yes. The key phrases are *comparable in structure* and *similar structurally*.

4.2a   TI—sentence 1; TS—sentence 2. The TI introduces the general subject of black African sculpture and modern artists. The TS states the specific subject of African primitive artists and Picasso.

4.2b   It lists all A (African) together and then all B (Picasso) together.

4.2d   Example: African Folk Sculpture and Pablo Picasso.

4.3a   It alternates A (West Germany) and B (Japan).

4.3b   No.

4.3c   Example: In many areas of social and industrial development, West Germany and Japan have made remarkable progress since World War II.

4.4a   TI—Introduces the general subject of Christianity and Islam
TS—Specifies sharing of beliefs and practices
AB—Combined example of both religions

A–E1—Christianity
B–E1—Islam
A–E2—Christianity
B–E2—Islam
R—Restates the subject of shared beliefs between Christianity and Islam

4.4b
Both Christian	and Muslims
Christian	holy book
Muslim	holy book
code of ethics	Christians
Muslim	daily guidance

4.4c TS—. . .*two faiths share*. . .
R—. . .*shared heritage of Christianity and Islam*.

4.5a It alternates A (Puerto Rican) and B (Southern Blacks).
4.5b The comparisons are stated in reverse order for subject B.
4.5c Yes. The key word is *skills*.
4.5d TI, TS / A–E1, A–E2, A–E3, A–E4, A–E5; B–E1, B–E2, B–E3, B–E4, B–E5 / R.

5.1a *however*; *On the other hand*; *In contrast*.
5.1b It alternates A (large university) and B (small college).
5.1c TS / A–E1, B–E1, A–E2, B–E2, A–E3, B–E3 / R.

5.2a (2) is best. (1) is too general and points out only one of the differences. (3) suggests that the purposes are different, but the paragraph states that the purposes are similar.
5.2b Example: British and American Universities.
5.2c It alternates A (British) and B (American).
5.2d Similarities: aims

federal support

Differences: size

specialised studies

support of private schools

support of students

5.3b

THE OBJECTIVE TEST	THE ESSAY EXAM
large number of questions	a few questions
true-false or multiple choice	essay form
detailed information	general concepts
unrelated questions	analytical and compositional skills
encourages guessing	guessing is reduced

5.5a   It alternates A and B examples.

5.5b   This is a matter of opinion. It frequently depends on the subject matter being discussed.

5.5c   TS / A–E1, B–E1, A–E2, B–E2, A–E3, B–E3, A–E4, B–E4 / R.

6.1a   Word level: spelling and capitalisation

words are changed

Sentence level: phrases put in different order

modification revised

different verb structures chosen

length of phrases or sentences revised

Between sentences   punctuation

or paragraphs: transitional devices

rewriting awkward phrases or sentences

6.1b   Reasons for editorial change.

6.2a   TP, CP1, CP2, CP3, RP.

6.2b   Underline sentence 1 in the TP. Yes.

6.2c   It lists all A (Gandhi) examples together, followed by all B (King) examples.

6.2d   It lists all A examples, followed by all B examples.

6.2e   Underline sentence 1 in CP3. Yes.

6.2f   It alternates A and B.

7.1a   Comparison, contrast, and synthesis.
Example: A definition paragraph explains by comparing, contrasting, or synthesising.

7.1b   Sentence 5.

7.1c   Products made from man-made materials, as synthetic rubber.

7.1d   It summarises the main points which define a term.

7.2a   Yes, but to a limited extent. It is the topic sentence.

7.2b   They add detail to the definition.

7.2c   *Energy-producing process* and *all plant and animal life.*

7.3a   wooded area . . . unusually heavy and frequent rains.

7.3b   Wooded area. The sentences discuss the places where these wooded areas exist, the kinds of trees in them, additional characteristics of the trees and other growth in the areas.

7.3c   No, not only wooded area. The sentence ties the two ideas together through the use of *luxuriant growth* and *rainfall.*

7.3d   They discuss a particular rain forest, El Yunque.

7.3e Through such phrases as *average rainfall 180 inches per year* and *trees, plants, greenery*, etc.

7.4a *No fixed homes* and *move regularly*.
7.4b Gypsies might be another example for some countries.
7.4c For the terminator to be effective, it must also fit your developer.

7.5 2, 1, 3, 5, 4, 6.
7.5a Sentence 1 introduces the term; no other sentence does, but all refer to it. Sentence 2 tells where the word comes from and indicates in a general way how it differs from any English equivalent. Sentence 3 gives one special quality conveyed by the term. Sentence 4 adds another quality which because of the *also* must follow 3. Sentence 5 expands on 4. Sentence 6 is the only sentence which summarises all the qualities.
7.5c Courageous behaviour and earthy sexuality. Sentence 1.
7.5d Sentences 2 and 3 to sexuality; 4 and 5 to courageous behaviour.
7.5e *also*.
7.5f Summarises principal qualities in the concept.

8.1a Yes. Paragraphs.
8.1b Sentence 5.
8.1c Our feeling is that the emphasis on *purpose* makes it difficult for students to concentrate on organisation. It is very difficult to generalise about what is exciting or persuasive; what interests one person may not excite another.
8.1d We hope so.

8.2a Examples.
8.2b Sentence 3.
8.2c They are likely to offend persons or cause them to evaluate you negatively if they consider them inappropriate to the situation in which they are used. There is some social consensus about when one can use language of this type even though such decisions are very arbitrary.

8.3a Use of first person. Style which sounds more spoken than written, e.g., use of contractions, direct quotations, etc.
8.3b Sentence 1. *Fall into three categories.*
8.3c Example: Types of Politicians
Three Kinds of Politicians

8.4a

CLASSES OF PEOPLE	TYPES OF VEHICLES
the economy minded	small, lightweight cars
the young	sports models
the middle-aged, middle class	big, sleek cars
the rich	luxury cars

8.4b   Examples:
service men   vans
oil delivery men   tankers
8.4c   Example: The Car Industry and the Buyer

8.5a   The final sentence.
8.5b   Vocational guidance; laboratory experiments involving animals; human neurosis.
8.5c   *in common.*

9.1   British university academic obligations of 3 types   1

lectures   2

tutorials   3

examinations   4

students prepare themselves by means of lectures, tutorials, and examinations   5

9.3a   It introduces the main subject—plagiarism—and defines it.
9.3b   Paragraph 1.
9.3c   Plagiarism by accident, by ignorance, and by intention.
9.3d   Sentence 1.
9.3e   Classification.
9.3f   Definition.
9.3g   Paragraph 2. Probably not. It is not very specific.
9.3h   Acknowledgement. The final paragraph.
9.3i   Yes. It refers back to the first paragraph with reference to the importance of giving proper credit for ideas.
9.3j   Yes. Discussion of the various types of plagiarism and definitions of these types.

10.1b   A frame controls or confines space.
10.1c   Sentence 9, colour; 7, perspective; 6, light.
10.1d   It intensifies his vision, and enables him to see the significance of the focus more clearly.

10.2a   1564 and 1616. They control or confine the events discussed in the paragraph.
10.2b   Lyric and narrative poetry; historical drama; comedies, and tragedies or tragi-comedies. It gives relationships between dates and literary types, which aids the reader's memory.
10.2c   Yes. A chronological listing is easier to remember than a random order.

10.3a   Sentence 2. *Athens...Babylon...led...across.*
10.3b   *Consuming...spreading.*

10.3c Yes, it refers back to *controversial figure* through such key words as *conqueror* and *hero*, and naming children after him but also instilling fear through his name.

10.3d Primarily, it presents movement in geographical space.

10.4 2, 7, 8, 1, 9, 10, 5, 6, 3, 4.

10.4b The developers follow a pattern of identifying the country first, followed by a sentence giving a date for writing in that country. To reverse that order would make the transitions very awkward.

10.5a Perhaps sentence 3, but sentence 4 makes it clear.

10.5c Egypt   2400 B.C.
Caspian Sea
Asia Minor
Greece   1000 B.C.
Sicily
France   600 B.C.
Rome   100 A.D.
Germany   200 A.D.
England
America   17th and 18th centuries

10.5d (1) Space
(2) Although the chronology of the paragraph is the same, no dates are given. There is a much clearer sense of space.

10.5e (1) Time
(2) Although places are mentioned or indirectly indicated, the dates become much more important in this paragraph.

10.5f We feel the first is perhaps most interesting, but any one of them might serve useful purposes.

11.1a Introduces the subject of safe water for modern cities. You might think that the subject of the paragraph is expenditures.

11.1b Further specifies that the subject is water. Indicates that the paragraph will discuss a two-step or three-step process for water purification.

11.1c The additional sentences expand, clarify, and illustrate the steps in the process.

11.1d *Water purification . . . city.*

11.1e No. If the order of the steps in the process were changed, something quite different might result. The main purpose of a process paragraph is to present steps in precisely the order necessary to bring about the desired result, in this example pure water.

11.2a The final sentence.

11.2b Seven. The first part of the paragraph, *first, second, third*; in the second part of the paragraph *first, then, These . . . result, Finally.*

11.2c It is a modulator or transition sentence. Moves the reader from technological changes to socio-economic-cultural changes.

11.2d It summarises the process of industrialisation and brings the paragraph to a satisfying conclusion.

11.4a It is the topic sentence.

11.4b It summarises the steps in the process.

11.4c It refers to what is to follow; it is a transition sentence. It indicates that additional steps in the process sometimes take place as suggested in sentence 2.

11.4d Cheese would probably not be produced.

11.4e *universal foods, varies only slightly.*

11.5a It is easier to keep several points in mind by grouping, or classifying them.

11.5b It is the first step in the process. It is an example of long-range planning.

11.5c It is an additional step in the process. *Assigned readings.*

11.5d It is an additional step in the process. *Throughout the year* refers back to *end of year examinations.*

11.5e Yes. Key words are *final examinations* and *year-long process.*

12.1a TP, time, space, process, process, RP.

12.1b Paragraph 1. Probably not. Because people had been living in the 'new world' 25,000 years before Columbus.

12.1c *Pre-* meaning before; *Columbian* is the adjective form of Columbus. It means before Columbus arrived.

12.1d Similar to type 4.

12.1e Climate and search for food.

13.1a Sentences 3, 4, and 5.

13.1b Sentence 1.

13.1c It is a topic sentence which indicates that the paragraph is going to give causes for the number of Americans killed in car accidents.

13.1d It is a terminator which restates in a dramatic way the final cause listed in sentence 5. It concludes the paragraph effectively by making the reader think of the implications of the statement.

13.2a It introduces the subject and indicates that three causes will be discussed.

13.2b Groups of people became separated from each other; interaction with foreign cultures; rapidly expanding technology and communications.

13.2c The phrase covers the three reasons listed in the paragraph.

13.2d Key words are *all languages change.*

13.3a Examples: poor study habits
too much social life
poor budgeting of time
poor class attendance
failure to hand in assignments on time
ineffective written assignments

13.3b An effective terminator would include reference to causes of dismissal from college, especially those within the student's control.

13.3c Sentence 1 states the effect. Sentence 3 states one cause. The student is expected to write additional causes.

13.3d Sentences 2 and 4 are transitional sentences suggesting the types of causes mentioned in sentences 3, 5, 6, and 7.

13.4a Sentence 6: *But in addition to these factors...*

13.4b We think not. In fact, it is difficult to take the paragraph seriously, for the sentence refers to little that has been discussed. It relates most to fatigue as a cause, but the reference is not clear enough to be a good terminator.

13.4c It seems to lack a conclusion and gives quite a lot of information that is already known to the reader.

13.5a Sentence 1. Yes.

13.5b It refers back to sentence 1: *society itself...producing... distortions...illness...instability.*

13.6a working available people long hours
use of women and children
population growth, especially immigration.

13.6b No. Immigration receives more emphasis.

13.6c Transition between lesser causes to most important cause.

14.2a It introduces the subject of small businesses and bankruptcy.

14.2b The final sentence generalises on the examples given in the paragraph and reaches a conclusion beyond what is possible from the observable facts.

14.2c They provide examples illustrating the complexity and change characteristic of modern business, and examples of small businesses being driven out by large concerns.

14.2d Key phrases might include: ...*victims...shifting economy;... fate of dissolution; taken over by a large store...more distant locations;...corner grocer's...gone to the nationally owned supermarket;...large chain;* etc.

14.3b Bad.

14.3d Key words might include *evening news, news broadcast, gloom, war, violence,* etc.

14.4a The final sentence.

14.4b The final sentence generalises about the importance of water to man, the first merely indicates that there is a lot of water on earth. The final sentence refers back to the first through *water*, of course, but also to man—dweller on the land.

14.5a Sentence 1.

14.5b Sentence 4.

14.5c Sentence 5.

14.5d It combines both elements—words and grammar—into a final or revised generalisation.

14.6a Education as a means of social control and its rapid growth in the past two decades.

14.6b Formal education becomes predominant and an occupational group of teachers comes into existence.

15.1   Time, space, Definition, Classification, Example, Generalisation.